THERE ARE NO BOUNDS

THERE ARE NO BOUNDS

WALLY NOEL

AuthorHouse™ LLC
1663 Liberty Drive
Bloomington, IN 47403
www.authorhouse.com
Phone: 1-800-839-8640

© 2014 Wally Noel. All rights reserved.

No part of this book may be reproduced, stored in a retrieval system, or transmitted by any means without the written permission of the author.

Published by AuthorHouse 08/26/2014

ISBN: 978-1-4969-3695-0 (sc)
ISBN: 978-1-4969-3694-3 (hc)
ISBN: 978-1-4969-3696-7 (e)

Library of Congress Control Number: 2014915489

Any people depicted in stock imagery provided by Thinkstock are models, and such images are being used for illustrative purposes only.
Certain stock imagery © Thinkstock.

This book is printed on acid-free paper.

Because of the dynamic nature of the Internet, any web addresses or links contained in this book may have changed since publication and may no longer be valid. The views expressed in this work are solely those of the author and do not necessarily reflect the views of the publisher, and the publisher hereby disclaims any responsibility for them.

Wally

a boy
watching carefully his parents
knowing but not yet knowing
that something was not quite right

grandparents
giving time and attention
feeding both body and soul
already wounded by neglect

random families
taking him in
sometimes with good intentions
but never really becoming family

a teen
struggling in school
knowing that whatever
other kids had
he did not

a dropout
who sensed that what
he needed to learn
would not be found in school

an enlisted man
hoping the Coast Guard
would help him find his place
and teach him skills

a husband
taking the leap into
marriage and fatherhood
all at once

a salesman
selling whatever he could
to whomever would buy
in nowhereville Kansas

a broker
finding success figuring
how to make money
for himself and others

a father
raising his children and
giving them everything
that he never had

a pizza man
stores sprouting like mushrooms
and making his fortune
"extra large" thank you

a rancher
with international flair
steers from Italy
improving the lot

a restaurateur
Out of Bounds the place
to see and be seen
eating, drinking and being merry

a lover
finding "the one" and
jetting away on the Concorde
after the vows

a collector
of homes, art, furniture
jewelry, cars
all the best money can buy

a philanthropist
giving to causes
making lives easier
and the world a better place

Wally
smart, motivated, energetic
tenderhearted, funny,
complicated, bossy
living an amazing life

—Susan Humphrey

Acknowledgments

Accolades to Susan Humphrey, my ghostwriter and trusted adviser.

To Frank Vaught, my buddy who kept after me for years to share my unique life. He kept repeating, "You need to write a book!"

To my beloved wife, Robin, whom I lost to cancer at the young age of forty-seven. She was my love, friend, and business partner for twenty-one years. She gave me the encouragement to pursue the business ventures I researched.

My sincere gratitude to my family and many friends for their heartfelt loyalty and encouragement.

Thanks to Kurt North for his help and guidance on this manuscript.

AuthorHouse for their support and feedback to bring this book to fruition.

Mine is the story of a person without a formal education who persevered and built a highly successful business career.

My advice to any person is this: If there is any way you can get a formal education, please do. However, if you can't, a lack of education doesn't mean you won't be able to succeed. Work hard, believe in yourself, and follow your dreams.

Chapter 1

It was a hot July day, with a temperature in the nineties and the humidity to match. *This is not for me. I don't want to be here!* I remember it as if it were yesterday, and the memories of the shoe factory in Sweet Springs, Missouri, flash before my eyes. I stood in an assembly line on a shoe-shank machine, hammering nails into the soles of shoes hour after mind-numbing hour. The air was dank with the smell of wet leather and thick with shoe-dye mist, which painted all of us dark brown. I watched my coworkers move like robots. Men who were in their thirties looked decades older, themselves tanned like shoes. I knew there had to be more to life than this. I thought, *You chose to work in this shoe factory over school.* Yes, I did.

I was seventeen when I quit high school during my sophomore year. I was in and out of so many schools during my childhood that I lost count. My parents put me in a foster home in Kansas City, Missouri, when I was entering tenth grade. The school was in an affluent area, and the students there were farther ahead than we had been at the schools in Sweet Springs, where I grew up. The school required me to take a test, and the school administrators determined that I was behind and put me back a grade. I was tired of feeling embarrassed and not fitting in. I didn't have the right clothes or shoes, and I never had spending money, like the other kids did. When the school held me back, I felt humiliated even further. Worse, my father came after a few months and returned me to Sweet Springs, but now I was back in the ninth grade instead of the tenth grade with my friends. I was not willing to repeat the ninth grade, so I quit school and took the first job I could find. I had no home to go to. I was fortunate that the parents of my best friend, Jerry Burnett, took me in and gave me a room to live in while I worked. They treated me like one of their own children. At least when I got paid, I could buy my own clothes and have some spending money, but I was miserable at the shoe factory and knew I had to find a way out.

I was born Wallace R. Noel on March 22, 1933, in Marshall, Missouri. My father chose to name me after a well-known comedian, Wallace Berry, who happened to be a heavy drinker like my father. I never cared for the name, so I encouraged friends to call me Wally. It was obvious to nearly everyone in our little town that my parents were not suited to be parents. Both my parents were more often drunk than sober and seldom kept my sister and me for any length of time. I knew at a young age that I never wanted to be like them. My parents were destructive to themselves and to each other. Drunken brawls were a regular occurrence, and when my father went to work, my mother entertained her drunken friends in our home. I knew there had to be a better life, and I planned to find it!

Before I was school age, my sister, Geraldine, and I were shuffled back and forth to grandparents, aunts and uncles, and even foster homes. My parents separated me from my sister at an early age. As young as I was, I always tried to protect my sister, and it broke my heart when my parents tore us apart. I remember the thoughts that flooded by mind: *I am not wanted by my parents. They don't care about me!* I'm sure this rejection was why I was so shy and ashamed of who and what I was.

When my parents did take us, we moved from town to town and school to school. There was no sense in making friends, as we never stayed in one place for long. The only feeling of love or care that I experienced came from my grandparents and other relatives, and I thank God for them. The only birthday gifts I can remember receiving as a child came from my grandparents, never my parents.

I was a kid on my own, surviving the best I could wherever I happened to be living. My grandparents were the closest thing I had to call family. My grandfather was the police chief in Sweet Springs, and my grandmother was a homemaker. They were good people, and I wished I could live with them permanently. Unfortunately, after a few weeks or months, my parents would reappear and take my sister and me back with them until their lives once again spiraled out of control, and then they'd dump us with whomever would agree to take us.

One summer, when I was about eight, I was playing outside with my friend Jerry. There was a grain elevator close by, and my grandparents had told me to stay away from it. Grain elevators are extremely hazardous, even for experienced adults who work in them. On this day, however, someone had left a door on the side of the silo open, and Jerry and I could not resist the temptation to explore and take a look inside. We stepped into the silo to look around. When our eyes adjusted to the darkness, I spotted the ladder elevator, and we decided to ride it to the top. I hit the on button, and up we went.

There Are No Bounds

When we got to the top, which was seven or eight stories up, we could see that the silo was divided into three sections. We got off the elevator and stepped onto a wooden platform that covered one of the sections, which was full of grain. We were having a great time, running around the platform hooting and hollering, when Jerry took off running. It was dark on the other side of the silo, and when I chased after Jerry, I didn't see that he had run across a two-by-twelve-foot plank suspended over an empty grain tube. Unaware of the plank, when I ran after him, I stepped out into thin air. With a seven-story drop, I knew I was a goner, but as I fell, a three-inch pipe used to vent gases from the grain caught me under my left armpit. I dangled above the darkness, petrified. I knew there was no one to save me, so I would have to do it myself. I slowly pulled myself along the pipe until I was able to reach the side and got one arm on the platform. I knew that to get onto the platform, I'd have to get my other arm up and let go of the pipe. In one of the scariest moments of my life, I let go and hauled myself to safety. Jerry and I quickly left the grain elevator and never told a soul what had happened. *I knew I had gotten a lucky break; I would have been just an ink spot on the floor if I had fallen. I had an instinct for survival and an unconscious understanding that anything I did, I would have figure out for myself.*

My parents divorced at some point, but since I didn't live with them, I have no idea when. Memories sometimes surface when least expected. I remember one incident in particular. My dad's girlfriend, Melba, and her parents had a cabin on the lake, and they would go out there to party and get drunk. One time, my dad took me with them, and I got a job rowing fishermen around the lake to make some spending money. I went out with jeans, no shoes, and no shirt. I came in from rowing on the lake that day, tied the boat up, and saw that my dad and Melba were fighting. My dad grabbed me by the arm and dragged me down the road to the highway. He flagged a Greyhound bus down. "Let's go! Let's go, Wally!" my father yelled. I can still hear him in my head.

I must have been nine or ten years old, and the memories are as vivid as if the events occurred yesterday. I remember the huge Greyhound bus as my father pushed me onto it. The bus went into downtown Kansas City, Missouri, to a large bus station where there were tons of people. I was barefoot and shirtless. I saw the faces of the people on the bus staring at us; their looks gave me a sinking feeling. I was embarrassed at how poor and pitiful we must have looked. My father was drunk; I only understood what to do because he pushed me in the direction he wanted me to go. Fortunately, where we were going and what happened next are blank in my mind, but I do remember my thoughts at that time. I promised myself that as soon as I was old enough, I would make sure I never had to live that way.

When my thoughts insist on bringing up my past, feelings and memories surface, and I think about what I learned from them. I remember the time I worked for my uncle Oscar, my dad's brother, at his pool hall. I believe working there played a big part in educating me about and preparing me for the real world. I stood watching and listening to men laughing and shooting pool in a smoke-filled pool hall. I didn't get a salary but received tips and spending money for oiling the floor and keeping the pool hall clean. Uncle Oscar liked me and made me the houseman. I also became very good at shooting pool. When I won, the house won. I learned how to work, I learned about running a pool hall, I learned plenty of things about people's lives that I probably shouldn't have, and I learned how to shoot pool, but the words rang in my ears: *This life is not for me!*

The long, tedious days at the shoe factory became months, and I knew I had to get away. At this point, I had lived in so many different houses that none of them was home. I did not know what my future held, but I did know one thing: there was nothing sweet about my life in Sweet Springs, Missouri, and I was impatient to create a different life for myself. I saw some coast guard promotions, and they looked exciting. I thought about them a lot and quickly made up my mind to start a new life. I went to Kansas City, Missouri, and enlisted. Although I was only seventeen, I lied about my age and told them I had already graduated from high school. They didn't ask to see any proof and let me sign up. There was no looking back, only forward. It was the biggest step I had ever taken and the smartest decision I ever made. It changed my life forever.

The coast guard sent me to Cape May, New Jersey, for boot camp, and after boot camp, they assigned me to duty aboard the United States Coast Guard cutter *Mackinaw*. I had no tangible skills, but I was not afraid to work and was a quick learner. The coast guard assigned me to damage control, meaning I was in charge of maintaining the ship; I learned to repair anything. The USCG cutter *Mackinaw* was a magnificent vessel stationed in Cheboygan, Michigan. The ship was an icebreaker, and it was our duty to keep lanes open through the ice so that freighters could get through. It was too big to get off the Great Lakes, because it couldn't get through the locks.

Many times, we had to tow freighters through the ice with a huge steel cable. We were a high target for the enemy in the Cold War era after World War II, because a huge amount of iron ore was shipped through the Great Lakes. Standing watch in subzero temperatures was routine; I spent many nights on deck sure that I would freeze to death before my shift was over.

The coast guard was now my life, and I was grateful. I was young and inexperienced but nevertheless excited to have a real job with pay, three square meals a day, and a place to sleep. It was the first time I felt I had a place where I belonged. The coast guard taught me things I would never have learned if I had not moved away from the town I had called home but, unfortunately, never was. I wanted to excel in every job given to me, and I was willing to do more than what my superiors asked of me. I was determined to make something of myself and was happy with my choice to be there. Jail would have been an improvement over the shoe factory, and the coast guard seemed like heaven.

I still thought about my baby sister, Geraldine, and what she must have been living through. Geraldine was three years, three months, and three weeks younger than I was. I felt responsible for her and remember picking her up from school when I was ten and fixing her mayonnaise-and-cracker sandwiches because there was nothing else to eat. To me, she was the sweetest and most beautiful little girl. My parents separated us, and I didn't know if they put her in a foster home or with a relative. No one ever told me. Her smile was all I had to remember her by, and it was branded in my mind. *Who is feeding her?* The thoughts hurt.

After a long day of duty, I often played baseball with the guys. One afternoon, during a game, I felt a sharp pain in my abdomen. I returned to the ship and lay down in my bunk. I pulled my knees to my chest. I was in awful pain, and there are no words to express how I felt. One of my buddies, Norm, walked in. "Hey, Wally, do you want to go into town tonight?" Norm was a funny guy and full of jokes, but I could not laugh at his jokes right then. The pain shot right through my right side, and I thought I would drop dead from it. I lay on my bunk and held my stomach; Norm could see something was terribly wrong.

I had never been sick, so I tried to play it off, but my friend could see the perspiration on my forehead. He pressed the back of his hand on my forehead. He yanked his hand back, "Man, you are burning up!" I knew by the tone of his voice that my condition must be serious. I could not stand on my own, so he lifted me up from the bunk and said, "I've got to get you to sick bay." I tried to resist, thinking it was just a bad stomachache, but the pain became excruciating.

An officer came and said, "Wally, are you really sick or trying to get out of duty?"

"No, I'm really sick; I'm hurting bad!"

The officer called a carryall, and they took me to the emergency room. I was on a table at the hospital; someone was cutting my shirt off. "What are you doing?" I faintly asked. A nurse was taking my blood pressure.

"Please, sir, be still."

My heart raced. I was not sure what was wrong with me, but I did as she said.

A tall man I assumed was the doctor leaned over me and tapped on my right side. I almost came off the table. The pain was the worst pain imaginable. Then he asked, "Wally, do you know why you're here?"

"No," I replied.

"Wally, I'm Dr. Wright. I'm going to do an emergency operation. Your appendix has ruptured, and peritonitis has set in. I have to operate immediately. Do you want me to call your parents?" It was difficult to stay focused on his voice.

"No, I don't know where my parents are; please call my grandparents." I knew my lips were barely moving, and the words seemed as if they were coming from somewhere else.

"Wally, hold on. I want you to talk to your grandparents. They need to know you are in the hospital," the doctor said. "Do it now!" He put the phone to my ear for only a few seconds. I could hear the doctor tell my grandparents, "Wally is in serious condition, but we'll do our best to take care of him." Those were the last words I heard.

I was in the hospital for seventeen days with tubes down my nose and throat. They were pumping the poison out of me into large vats. Later, my friend Norm told me that the doctor had told my grandparents they had not expected me to live, and neither had he.

Chapter 2

As time moved forward in the coast guard, I found each day new and exciting. I felt like a man, not a boy who desperately wanted to be away from poverty and the lack of food, love, and hope. I had no thoughts of my parents, but I did stay in contact with my grandparents, the only family I had.

Each day, I awoke with the expectation of having new things to learn. When I first was aboard the ship, the officers taught me duties I needed to become skilled in and eventually master. There are many things about operating a ship that most people have never heard of, and I hadn't either. One of the duties assigned to me was the bow watch. Maritime law says a ship has to maintain a bow watch even though it has sonar and radar. Bow watch at night when the temperature was twenty to thirty degrees below zero was tough duty. We smeared axle grease on our eyelids, nose, and lips to keep them from freezing shut and had to be tied to the ship with ropes around our waists. There was no footing on the icy deck, and that lifeline was all there was to prevent us from falling overboard to certain death.

For me, other undesirable duties included doing the laundry, red-leading pipes in the bilges, and chipping and repainting all things aboard the ship. Laundry duty meant washing, steaming, and pressing all the ship's laundry. We would red-lead pipes by lying on our backs and painting the miles of pipes that ran through the bilges. One of the most boring duties was chipping and repainting the ship. The officers usually assigned all of these duties to the new guys aboard ship. The point was to teach us to obey orders regardless. I noticed that if you kept your mouth shut and did a good job, you got less of these duties, but if you were a slacker, you were reassigned the worst jobs again and again. I became determined to do it right the first time and get rewarded with better duties.

Our boatswain's mate, Bill, known as Boats, could make our daily duties tough. He was the most versatile member of the coast guard's operational team and a master of seamanship. The boatswain is capable of performing almost any task in connection with ship maintenance. He supervises all personnel assigned to a ship's crew. He is like a foreman in a factory; he assigns duties and makes sure the crew completes them. He knows the ship like the back of his hand. When you first go aboard a ship, you have no knowledge of what it takes to run the ship. It is the boatswain's duty to assign everyone many different chores to teach them how a ship operates.

One of Bill's main concerns was the safety of the ship and his crew. Safety meant going over safety measures daily; our lives counted on it. Due to the seriousness of the need to follow rules, he often told catastrophic stories. Some stories like the story of the aft hatch, I will never forget. We were piped up on deck. We did not have to wait long before Bill marched around inspecting us as he moved up and down the row of men. We stood at attention until we heard him say, "At ease." While on deck, we listened attentively as he reminded us of the stupid things that had cost men's lives.

Norm and I made eye contact when Bill raised his voice louder than usual. He made sure he had all of our attention. He was one tough guy. We learned a lot from him but avoided his anger when we hadn't done things to his approval. Boatswain mates like Bill were no-nonsense men; we respected his knowledge and were eager to hear another story. "Who knows why there are so many hazard signs around the aft hatch?" Bill said loudly. Silence filled the deck; I could hear the swells against the side of the ship, and even they seemed to move quietly. Of course, I wanted to answer, but if I did not give the answer he expected, he would cut me down with words. I guess the other guys thought like me; they did not offer answers either. We stood without moving a muscle and waited for his answer.

"Okay, let's start with something simple," he snapped. He turned slightly to the left and then to the right, making eye contact with the crew. "One day just like today a few years ago, everything was running like it should. While towing a freighter ..." His words slowed; his voice was no longer loud. "While towing a freighter," he said, starting again, "one of the crew came up the ladder through the aft hatch, and at that precise moment, all the strain on the wire rope pulling the freighter made it break, and the cable flew across our ship. It sounded like a cannon. That wire rope cut that man in half! Did you hear me, men? In half!" He watched our faces—faces that reflected his feelings. The shock of what he had witnessed was still imprinted in his mind and was now in ours as well.

"Accidents happen, but only when you forget to pay attention to the rules of the ship! Never, never," he shouted, "never come up through a hatch on the afterdeck when we are towing. Is this understood?"

I could hear most of the crew say, "Yes, sir!" We went back to our duties and did not mention the story again. I think we all knew how hazardous our jobs could be. We knew our positions, and most of us were good at them.

Not long after that safety meeting, Norm and I, with a few other guys, were working on something on the dock with Bill, our boatswain. Did I mention that he was not a friendly guy? He gave us hell about nearly everything we did, even when he stood over us giving instructions. I can honestly say the men didn't like him much. We all wanted to be where he wasn't. I was standing next to him, watching nervously while the other guys followed his orders. In my peripheral vision, I saw a buoy swinging loose from the buoy tender docked next to us. The buoys used on the Great Lakes weighed over a ton. I jumped on Bill, pushing him down on the dock. The buoy swung over our bodies, and we rolled out of harm's way. My action was pure instinct; there was not a second to think about danger.

Bill and I were at a loss for words. After we got to our feet, the guys were in shock. One of the guys shouted, "Bill, that buoy missed you by an inch! Damn, Wally, you could have been killed with him!"

I could feel the adrenaline running its course through my body. It was true. I said, "Sorry, sir, about pushing you down."

I was brushing myself off a little when Bill said, "You saved my life, Wally." His voice was a little shaky, but I tried not to notice. After all, he was the boatswain. He stared at me as if meeting me for the first time. "Thank you," he said again.

We had all moved away from the unsecured buoy. "It was instinct, sir! Glad I could help." *What do you say to your boss when you just saved his life?* He had thanked me for my quick action, because there was no doubt that if I had not pushed him at that precise moment, he might have been dead. I had merely reacted, and from that day on, Bill treated me with favor, but he was still a tough son of a gun.

The coast guard was teaching me to be a man. I stayed so busy with my duties and was so eager to learn new things that my past thoughts became less and less frequent. I stayed focused on a better future. Time passed quickly, and my travels were enlightening. I saw things that lit up my mind and made me realize that all things were possible. When hanging around the ship, I'd share my thoughts and ideas on how to make things work better. My buddies would stop and say, "Man, Wally, where do you come up with these wild ideas?"

When the officers saw how I handled the helm, they trusted me with one of the most responsible duties on the bridge. The coast guard cutter *Mackinaw* did not have a wheel on the bridge; instead, it had a stick. The stick was delicate. The ship was 5,252 long tons and did not respond instantly. When moving that kind of tonnage through the water, you steer ahead of the ship. I got proficient at figuring out when to use the stick, and the officers called on me to steer the ship when we were in tight places.

After we docked in Chicago, my buddy Norm finished his duties and came looking for me. "Wally, let's go to the Loop!" His excitement was contagious. I'm sure the majority of the crew were excited to get off the ship.

"Sounds like a plan to me," I quickly answered. After three weeks on the ship, solid ground sounded good. I had my sea legs, but land was a welcome sight.

That evening, we lost count of how many bars we went in and out of. Although I was under the legal drinking age, we were in uniform, and no one questioned our age. Norm and I were like brothers, and we made lots of friends that we knew we would never see again. It was well into the night when Norm said, "Let's get a tattoo!" I saw the sign at the same time he did: TATTOOS. I had never been a drinker, so I am sure my judgment was impaired.

"Let's do that!" My words slurred, and my legs staggered through the door with Norm. Everything seemed so funny, and getting a tattoo at the moment sounded fearless. The next morning, I woke with the worst headache imaginable. I rubbed my eyes and my head. To my shock, I saw my arm bandaged from my wrist to my elbow. *What is wrong with my arm?* My head ached, and so did my arm. *What happened?* screamed in my brain. I nearly fell when I jumped out of my bunk. *So this is what a hangover is like.* I could not remember what I had done or where I had gone the night before. I knew Norm and I had had a lot to drink, but for the life of me, at that moment, the last night was a blank. I could not remember how I had gotten back to the ship or into my bunk. It seemed we must have had a good time—too bad I couldn't remember it. My arm throbbed in pain; I sat on the side of the bunk, doing my best to recall the previous night. *Did I fall?* I began pulling at the bandage, and when I saw blood on my arm, blood rushed to my head. I felt frightened and confused at the same time. With difficulty, I desperately tried to focus my eyes, blinking constantly to erase the cloud of confusion. Did I mention that my head ached? Oh man, I really needed some aspirin!

The bandage fell as if in slow motion, and I could clearly see that there on the swollen skin was a tattoo—a huge tattoo that covered my forearm. It was a big ship with three seagulls and a three-masted sailing vessel with *Wally* under the ship. *Horrified* is the best word to describe what I felt. I dressed quickly and went to find Norm. I found him up on deck, joking with some of the guys. "Norm!" I yelled. "What in the hell happened last night?" I stretched my arm out before him.

"Damn, Wally, why did you do that?" He was laughing, but I knew he was shocked to see how big the tattoo was. So were the other guys standing there in disbelief. "Wally, that is *big*!" Norm shook his head. I was still in shock; my arm ached.

"Where's yours?" I asked.

Norm's eyes rolled, and then he slowly rolled up his T-shirt sleeve. I wanted to sock him. All he got was a little rose. "A little rose?" I yelled. "It's so small!" "What the hell, Norm? You can't even see it." Most of the guys were laughing, but humor was not appropriate at the time. I had enough sense to know I was property of the United States Coast Guard, and that meant my body, including my arm, belonged to them. I knew this would be unacceptable.

While he and I argued back and forth about who was to blame, one of the officers saw the tattoo on my arm and reported me. I was called in and told I would have to go before a captain's mass—in laymen's terms, a court martial. The captain made me stand before the crew, officers, and himself. He laid into me like you wouldn't believe. He told me how dumb getting a tattoo was and said that I would live to regret it. I'm sure he could have put me in the brig. I guess he saw I was young and had made a stupid mistake, and he took mercy on me. The threat of a court martial was truly punishment enough. I made sure I wore long sleeves to hide that tattoo, no matter the weather, for the rest of my time in the coast guard.

The captain was right; I regretted that tattoo from the day I discovered it, and I did my best to keep it hidden. The three-masted sailing vessel with *Wally* written beneath it haunted me for years to come. *Drunk and* out of control ... I had visions of my dad and the stupid things he did when he was drunk. I was trying to get away from that life, not repeat it. I never again wanted to wake up in the morning to find I had done something stupid. I would never allow alcohol to control me; I couldn't!

While our ship was docked in Cheboygan, Michigan, I saw a lifestyle I had never been exposed to while growing up in Missouri. I saw yachts and riches that blew my mind. I couldn't believe anyone could have that much money and live that way, but I was inspired to have that lifestyle. Occasionally, our ship docked at Mackinaw Island, a small island located in Lake Huron between Michigan's upper and lower peninsulas. Mackinaw Island has been a tourist destination since the late 1800s, when the Grand Hotel was constructed. The Grand Hotel draws summer vacationers from all over the country, and many famous people, including presidents of the United States, have stayed there.

The island is beautiful and clean, and no cars are allowed on the island. When our ship docked there, I watched wealthy people living a lifestyle that I could only dream of having. Our ship was the lead ship for some of the yacht races that took place there, and I saw private yachts that I couldn't believe! Seeing this gorgeous place with beautiful, wealthy people enjoying their lives made a lasting impression. There was a world out there that I had never known existed. Now that I had seen it, I wanted that life too.

Even though I loved the cutter *Mackinaw* and knew it inside and out, my enlistment was nearing its end. The coast guard was good to me and taught me many valuable lessons. Looking forward to a new life out of the service, I now had to figure out how to take those lessons and turn them into a future.

I joined the coast guard at seventeen a kid with few skills, no direction, or much hope that I could find a better life for myself. I was discharged three years later a young man who had mastered many skills and learned discipline and accountability in the process. For the first time in my life, I discovered that I could be rewarded for hard work and doing things right the first time. I had never gotten anything but criticism from my dad growing up, so the idea of the value of accomplishment was new to me. I learned that if I always did more than what was asked of me and to do it well, the reward would follow. "Dream big and aim high" was a belief born during my time in the coast guard and one that has served me well throughout my life.

Chapter 3

Immediately after getting out of the coast guard, I searched for work and, luckily, found that an auto plant in Detroit, Michigan, was hiring. Americans were well on the way to becoming a motorized society. The Depression and the halt in auto production during World War II had slowed the growth of America's car culture, but after the war, the number of cars in the United States nearly doubled, increasing from thirty-nine million to seventy-four million. Most American families now owned one car.

I worked on an assembly line at General Motors, installing car jacks into the trunks of cars. The work was hard, and my hands were constantly bruised and cut having very little time as the cars moved along the assembly line to jam each car jack into its small space. Nevertheless, I worked as many hours as I could, picking up overtime and double time for working nights, weekends, and holidays. I lived in a boarding house, and while I was making enough money to support myself, I was lonely and homesick. I wanted to go home. When I heard that one of my buddies from the service was heading to Kansas, I quit my job and hopped a ride with him back to Sweet Springs, Missouri.

My grandparents were happy to see me, as I had been home only once in my three years in the coast guard, and they allowed me to move back in with them. My parents were no longer in the area, and frankly, I didn't know or care where they were. The only real parents I ever had were my grandparents, and I was glad to be back with them. I immediately started doing odd jobs around town and at neighboring farms. I was young, strong, handy, and a hard worker, so I had no trouble keeping busy. I found a job selling magazines, and while the job was commission only, they provided me with a much-needed car, so I took the job.

Selling magazines to farmers was no easy task. In those days, money was hard to come by, and farmers were not about to part with the little they had. After several frustrating weeks of being turned down again and again, I had an idea. Every farm I called on had things lying around the property—junk! I thought the farmers might be willing to trade some of that junk for a magazine subscription. Sure enough, they gladly parted with tires, batteries, copper wire, and even eggs. They had plenty of commodities to trade for their magazines, so I took what I could get and resold the products for more than the subscription would have cost. Although I made enough to have spending money, I knew that I could never make enough to support myself in the long run. I thought that air-force security work would give me more opportunities, so once again, I joined the military.

Air-force boot camp was in Cheyenne, Wyoming. I had been to boot camp for the coast guard and knew the drill, so this wasn't hard for me. One weekend, some of the guys and I went to a rodeo during the Cheyenne Frontier Days. While there, I ran into a pretty woman named Delores. She was nice and friendly, and I was interested. She told me she was a hairdresser in Greeley, Colorado, so I quickly made an appointment to get my hair cut. There was something about her; we just clicked. I called her Lorrie, and the name stuck. I actually think she liked the name Lorrie better than Delores. We began dating and, within a few months, got married.

Lorrie had a six-year-old daughter named Sandy, and at the time, it was hard to make ends meet for a single mother, and consequently, Sandy was living in a foster home. Once we married, Lorrie was able to bring Sandy home, and in less than a year, our son Larry was born. I was happy to be married and have my own family, but I was only twenty-one, and the sense of responsibility was enormous. I tried my best to be a good father and work my fingers to the bone, if necessary, to give them the necessities of life: food on the table, a roof over their heads, and clothes on their backs. Never would my children go hungry and eat crackers and mayonnaise, as my little sister and I had.

I had not had contact with my parents since I joined the coast guard, and many nights, I thought about letting my parents know that I was a father and that they had grandchildren. I wanted them to know how seriously I took my responsibilities, but I couldn't bring myself to call them. When I'd lived in foster homes, other kids' parents had come to see them, but mine never had. I'd always felt unwanted, and I still get choked up when I think about it. My parents only cared about where their next drink was coming from, never about my sister or me. I believe my drive came from that experience; I would never be that kind of parent, and my children would never know want or neglect, as I had.

There Are No Bounds

After boot camp, the air force transferred me to Victorville, California. Lorrie, the kids, and I had to live on the air-force base. This was a struggle from the first day. The money wasn't bad, but our living conditions were awful in Victorville. We had to sleep in the men's barracks, and I had to have someone guard Lorrie and Sandy while they were in the shower and bathrooms, to ensure their privacy and safety. This was not a good environment for my family; it was difficult on us all. We tried to move off base, but there were absolutely no accommodations in the whole city. The air force saw that this living situation was a struggle for my family and, in less than a year, gave me an honorable discharge for hardship.

After my discharge, we needed a place to stay. Fortunately, Lorrie had friends living in Compton, California, who allowed us to visit them and stay at their home. While there, I worked odd jobs until one day, Lorrie's friend Bob gave me a Fuller Brush suitcase, filled it with samples, and told me I could keep whatever orders I sold. "Good luck," Bob said. He told me that he had not been able to sell anything in the area he gave me. I received no training, because I was not really working for the Fuller Brush Company; I was working for Bob, who was just lending me part of his territory. The Fuller Brush Company sold floor brushes, brooms, household cleaning products, polishes, and waxes. I looked in my suitcase at what he had given me, and off I went, door-to-door. The Fuller Brush Company was well known at the time, and we put stickers on all the doors in the area, announcing when we would be calling. Generally, homeowners invited me into their homes when I called, and then I proceeded to show what I had. The company's quality products and unconditional guarantee helped me make sales, and I had great luck selling. Bob was impressed.

I had to do whatever it took, and it was honest work. One day, feeling excited about my new adventure in sales, I knew I would have a good day. Funny things happen when you go selling door-to-door. That day, I knocked on many doors with no answer but still felt that I would make more sales than I had the day before. It was a beautiful day with perfect weather. I remember thinking as I walked up a long walkway, *This is sure a long walk to such a small house.* As I got closer to the porch, I noticed that someone was peeking out the front window. The sun was in my eyes, but I was sure I saw the curtain in the window move. I thought the person would probably ignore my knocking, but instead, after the second knock, a woman quickly opened the door. As I said, the sun had blurred my vision a little, but my vision was clear as I saw that she was butt naked. A lump in my throat prevented me from speaking for a second. "Ma'am!" I was speechless. What seemed like minutes of silence was probably seconds. She had a nice figure; I can't remember her face. I felt embarrassed—I'm not sure if for her or me—so I handed her my brochure and said, "Have a good day, ma'am!" I turned around and moved as quickly as my feet could walk back down that long driveway. At twenty-one with a wife and two kids, I was scared and knew to walk away.

Several weeks later, in another neighborhood, I knocked on a door, and a young, attractive woman answered the door in a black lace negligee. I'm sure my eyes were as big as dollars. Even though this was the second time something like this had happened, I was caught off guard and didn't know what to do. Her smile was inviting, but a voice in my head said, *Walk away, Wally,* and I did. There was no way I was crossing the threshold of that house! I told Bob what had happened, and we laughed for days about the unexpected education I was getting by doing door-to-door sales.

I was doing well enough working Bob's territory, but the job was not really mine. Bob was just giving me work to do and a way to earn a little money until I was able to find my own job. Lorrie and I didn't want to overstay our welcome and knew we needed to get a place of our own, so in a short while, it was time to move on.

I found a job with General Motors on an assembly line in South Gate, California. This time, my job was to wash the car windows inside and out on one side of the cars. I worked my regular shift and took any nights, weekends, and holidays that I could. Every week or two, I had to replace the jeans I wore, as jumping in and out of cars all day ripped the backside to shreds. Those cars came down the assembly line just three minutes apart, so speed was important, and I always kept up. I was making more money that I had ever made in my life. I paid off all our debts and our car. In a week, I earned more than twice the money I had in a month in the air force. I felt that I was doing well—but then General Motors' union went on strike for seven months, and my job vanished. Life can change on you when you least expect it. Overnight, I was once more out searching and taking any job I could find.

It didn't take long before we were out of money. I sometimes went out at night and shot rabbits to bring home to my family for dinner.

There Are No Bounds

I grew up hunting, and I'm a pretty good shot. I'd go down by the highway with my .22-caliber gun and wait for cars to pass. Rabbits freeze when they see headlights, and you can see their eyes shining. I'd shoot them in the head and skin them on the spot, leaving their innards and skins for the coyotes. I'd also try to catch fish to bring home, usually carp. They don't taste all that great and are full of bones, but the fish are large and have a lot of meat on them. Better that than letting my family go hungry.

Once, I was on the highway, coming home from an odd job, when I ran out of gas. I hiked to the nearest gas station, but I had no money. I told the owner of the station my problem and asked if he could give me a gallon of gas (at the time, the cost was around thirty cents a gallon) and promised I would bring the money in the next day. He looked at me and said, "You aren't a regular customer here, and now you want me to give you gas?" I tried to explain again that I just needed a gallon and that I would be back the next day to pay him, but he refused. I couldn't believe it. I felt entirely humiliated that I was in this situation, and I knew he was figuring me for a loser. I have never forgotten that night and how ashamed I felt to not have thirty cents to my name.

When we couldn't pay our electrical bill, the electric company came out and shut off our electricity. Suddenly, we had no lights and no heat, with two little kids at home. I didn't know what to do, so I walked around the house until I spied the electrical box. I began to jiggle the box and discovered the cover was loose, so I yanked on it, and the darn thing came off in my hands. When I looked on the house I could see where three prongs were coming out of the electrical box. The three prongs were covered plastic sleeves, and I knew no electricity could flow through them. I looked at those prongs and saw they plugged right into the meter, and in less than five minutes, I turned our electricity back on. We never got another bill, as apparently the company never discovered my solution.

My next job was at Pacific Telephone and Telegraph, working as a station installer, crawling under homes to install phones and strapping on climbers to climb phone poles to install the wiring. Colored phones had just come on the market, and part of my job was to sell telephones. I talked people into buying phones for several rooms in their homes, and those homes were tiny. I was never a high-pressure salesman. Rather, I made the customers feel as if they needed two or three phones because that was what all their neighbors were buying, and they deserved to have them as well. I sold them a different-colored phone for each room, and they felt "uptown." People like to feel they are keeping up with the times and like to have what other people have.

The company gave me a truck and a large commercial area, but after seven or eight months, I asked for a transfer to Greeley, Colorado, so that Lorrie could move closer to her family. Lorrie was pregnant again and feeling lonely living so far from her parents. The company told me that I could transfer, and we packed up our belongings in my car and drove to Colorado. When we got to Greeley, I showed up to work only to find out the transfer had not gone through, and there was no job waiting for me. I suspect that someone gave my job to a friend or relative before I got there, but I couldn't prove it. I immediately found work in construction, plumbing, and concrete work. I worked well with my hands, as my time in the coast guard had taught me many talents. Even more important, as I would later find out, selling magazines, Fuller brushes, and colored telephones had taught me something new—sales.

We were renting a basement apartment from Gordon Mackey, who was the sales manager for Wynn's Friction Proofing; he was responsible for an area in Colorado. He had asked me several times to work for him on commission. I told him I could not afford to work on commission only; I had a family to take care of, which had increased with the birth of our son Michael. Finally, one day, he said he would give me a hundred dollars a week and commission. I took the job.

Wynn's Friction Proofing manufactured an oil treatment for automobiles, race cars, and airplanes. The company produced the additive in single-unit quantities for autos. While most of the salesmen were selling small cans to service stations, I started thinking, *Why not sell to larger users?* I figured that if the oil treatment was good for autos, it would also be good for trucks and tractors. I began selling to construction companies, trucking companies, and other large users. I would mix a gallon of Wynn's into a fifty-five-gallon drum of oil so that the large users could treat their equipment without having to mix it themselves. It made me realize that I not only was good at sales but also was a good problem solver. I sold such large orders of the fifty-five-gallon drums that Carl Wynn had me fly to California to see him at the Wynn's Friction Proofing Company plant. He was so excited about my sales production that he gave me the state of Kansas for my territory. I was excited! That promotion really made me think I was a salesman.

Lorrie and I packed up the kids and our belongings and headed to Kansas City to begin a new chapter of our lives. Lorrie never questioned my decisions and supported me, even though it meant leaving Greeley, Colorado. When we arrived, we rented a small home, and I immediately hit the road to start selling Wynn's Friction Proofing in the state of Kansas. While traveling back and forth from one town to another, I stopped at Leavenworth Prison, a medium-security penitentiary for male inmates, and got an order from them. They purchased friction proofing for all of the vehicles at the prison. When I went back to deliver their order, I stood watching guards escorting prisoners from the building. I saw a life that saddened my heart, and I wondered why anyone would commit a crime that would send him to a place like that. I could not wait to get out of there! I knew that many of the prisoners were people just like me—men who had been abused and neglected but had turned to crime as their way out. I was never tempted to go down that road. I wanted to be the opposite of my parents, especially my dad, and the desire to succeed burned within me.

I thought about my other commercial accounts and wondered what other government entities I could call on. Why not the armed forces, post offices, and municipalities? I thought about military installations and all the vehicles the military had. The sky was the limit! In my mind, I saw orders coming in for not thousands but millions of dollars. But how could I sell to the military? Go to Washington, DC? I realized that a retired president lived close by. President Truman's Library was a lot closer than Washington, DC, so I decided to roll the dice and see if he would give me an audience.

I called the library and asked the receptionist if it would be possible for me to see the former president. I told her I was a young businessman who wanted some advice on how to see the right people in Washington about my products. To my utter amazement, she asked President Truman, and he said he would see me. She asked me if 3:00 p.m. was all right. I, of course, said yes. She said, "Your name please," and I said, "Wally Noel." I was so surprised, I had trouble talking, but I thanked her for the appointment. I had a huge smile on my face. I couldn't believe that I had an appointment with the former president of this country.

I arrived in Independence, Missouri, for my appointment and pulled into the Truman Library parking lot. I was early. I sat in my car, thinking, *If you're going to dream, Wally, dream big.* The president's library was more than I had imagined. *This was my moment.* The receptionist asked me to wait on a sofa. In a short time, President Truman appeared and sat down on the sofa with me.

To be honest, I was scared, but it wasn't long before I relaxed. The president offered me his hand, and he gave me a firm handshake. There is no way to explain the feeling you get when you meet such an important person. He quickly put me at ease. He asked how he could help me. I told him that I had the Kansas territory for Wynn's Friction Proofing and was interested in introducing my products into the armed forces. "The product has proven itself in many tests to be very reliable in reducing friction in moving parts in any kind of vehicle. We would be willing to do tests in any type of vehicle at our expense. My problem is that I don't know whom to see in Washington," I said.

The answer I got from President Truman was a shocker! He said, "Young man, when you go to Washington, get yourself a great big suitcase and fill it with money. Every time you shake hands with someone, leave some money in his hand." I could hardly believe what I had just heard. I left the library with great respect for President Truman but knew I didn't have nearly enough money to follow his advice.

That day stands out in my mind and is one I will never forget. I can truly say President Truman did not put on airs or come off as a Washington bureaucrat. He treated me cordially, and I was in awe of him but did not feel intimidated. I left the meeting with President Truman with even more respect for him than I'd had before our meeting. Meeting with the former president of the United States was a giant step. After that day, I thought, *There are no bounds!*

I loved what I was doing, and my thoughts of expanding my business and career were forefront in my mind. Soon, however, my success as a salesman began to overtake my ability to buy enough product to service my customers. I needed to be able to buy boxcars full of Wynn's Friction Proofing, but I didn't have the capital to buy the product up front. I was able to hustle and sell to just about anyone who would listen to me, but I was not an experienced businessman, and I had no idea how to raise the money I needed. It soon became clear that I had bitten off more than I could chew. I didn't have a suitcase full of money for the Washington bureaucrats, nor did I have enough money to stay in business. There were no bounds for my ambition, but my resources limited me. There were plenty of things I needed to learn before I could be successful. I was getting a business education in real time.

I hadn't completed high school, and going to college was out of the question. I had to learn what I needed to learn on the job; I had no choice. However, I also know getting a diploma does not necessarily guarantee success. Trying, failing, and trying again is its own education. When I met President Truman, I knew if I kept knocking on doors and asking questions, eventually, I'd figure out how to survive in the business world.

Chapter 4

I went home and told Lorrie I had to leave Wynn's Friction Proofing. I had already tried to stay afloat with a $2,000 investment from a friend, but it wasn't enough. She never questioned my decision, as she knew I'd have something else going before long. I always kept my fears from Lorrie when things didn't go as planned. Inside, I was still a scared kid running away from my past. *I will never be like my dad, who left us without food and left me trying to figure out what I could scrounge for my little sister to eat so that she didn't go hungry.* I saw an ad in the paper for a sales job for Remington Rand typewriters. I knew nothing about the typewriter business, but I now had experience in sales, so I figured I'd go for it. Sure enough, Remington Rand hired me on the spot. I asked if they had a territory in Wichita, and they did. Again, we packed our children and our belongings into the car and drove in the night toward an uncertain future.

We settled into another tiny, furnished home, which wasn't too bad once we got rid of the bedbugs that were in residence when we got there. They made our first night in the house memorable, but not in a good way. Before we had unpacked, I was making my first calls, convincing whomever answered the door that he or she needed to own a Remington typewriter.

After several months, a friend of mine who had a piece of property told me that if I could find someone to help us raise the money to build a bowling alley, he would make me the manager. Now, that sounded like a big deal to me! I was young and naive. "Where do you go to get money for construction?" I asked. He told me that I could call on investment banking firms, which generally had the money to develop projects if they were interested in them. My friend was leaving the finding-the-money part of this project to me. Little did I know that what came next would change my life.

I started looking around and found the name Melbourne and Cochran Investment Banking. I got an appointment and, on that day, walked into a meeting where several men were sitting at a long conference table. One of those men was Don Small. I had on my best (cheap) brown suit, but I held my head high. I shared with the gentlemen that investing in a bowling alley would bring in a good amount of revenue. Bowling alleys were becoming popular at this time, and we had a great location. Mr. Small, I could see, was paying close attention to what I had to say. He was in his midforties, confident, charismatic, and well-tailored. I was impressed. Toward the end of the meeting, Mr. Small said, "Wally, you're wasting your time." I thought they weren't interested or didn't like my presentation. Mr. Small either read my mind or saw the disappointed look on my face, because he quickly said, "No, don't take it wrong. Here's my card. I'd like you to come see me at my office tomorrow."

The next day, I went to his office, and after we talked awhile, he said, "Wally, I'm going to hire you!"

"To do what?" I answered, somewhat surprised.

He said, "To be an investment banker!"

"I don't even know what that is, Don," I replied. I hoped my lack of knowledge and inexperience would not affect his thinking.

Don said, "It won't take you long, Wally."

I asked, "What would I do?"

We continued to talk, and he told me that I would call on banks, institutions, and wealthy individuals and offer them securities on our municipal bond list. I didn't know a security from a typewriter, but I figured I could probably sell them; however, I did admit that I didn't know what a municipal bond was. *He might as well have been speaking a foreign language. I did not let on that I had mainly worked with my hands. I listened with interest. I was eager to learn what he was offering.*

Don's voice was precise; it was obvious to me that he had made the decision that I was the man he wanted by his side. He spoke with self-assurance. "Wally, you can do this, and I'm going to help you." *I knew at that moment he trusted me. He saw something in me, and that motivated me to believe I could do anything.* "I'm going to give you eastern Kansas as a territory. You'll travel that territory and sell securities, meeting with bankers, insurance companies, and individuals who buy these types of securities—get acquainted with them and their needs."

I was paying attention, and my thoughts flowed out of my mouth as soon as I opened it. "Don, I already have a problem—my car won't make it. It barely makes it around town!" I knew this was a great opportunity, but I had to be honest. I did not want to start something that my car could not finish. Don walked over to his desk chair and sat down. He fumbled with a notepad and looked me in the eye.

"That's not a problem, Wally; my mom is getting ready to trade in her Buick. I'll keep her car and lend it to you until you get on your feet and get established."

Without hesitation, I said, "Okay!" I could barely hide my excitement; I felt ten feet tall. I was twenty-five years old, and I was now in the investment business. My real life got started that day, and Don Small was the instrument that changed my life.

Don lent me his mother's tan-and-gold Buick (the nicest car I had ever driven), gave me the list of securities his company had to offer, and talked to me for a couple of hours about the business of selling securities. It was clear that the only way to learn this business was to get out there and do it. All I knew as I headed out the door on my first day was that I would pick a highway and drive until I reached a town with a bank; then I would go in and start selling.

I drove northeast from Wichita on Highway 35. Thirty miles from Wichita was a town named El Dorado. It was a large enough town to have a bank, so I drove into town, parked my "new" car in front of the First National Bank, and, trying to look confident, walked in. I didn't know whom I should see, but I walked up to the front desk, introduced myself, and asked, "Who buys your bonds?"

"That would be Mr. Kilgore, the bank's president," the woman answered. I asked if I could see him, and she took me to his office.

"I just went to work for Small and Company," I said. "This is my first day, and you are my first call in my brand-new job, and I really don't know what I'm doing, but I've got a list of bonds I'd like you to look at."

Mr. Kilgore took the list of bonds from me and saw two $10,000 maturities (blocks of bonds) for the El Dorado School District. He looked up at me and said he would take one of each. I went cold. I was excited to make a sale but had no idea what to do next. I asked if I could call the office, and Mr. Kilgore let me use the phone on the desk.

When Don Small answered the phone, he was flabbergasted. In my first hour on the job, I had sold $20,000 worth of bonds. He instructed me to tell Mr. Kilgore that the bonds' sale was confirmed and that I would get back to him. Don told me to get back to the office right away. When I arrived, we both got into Don's car and headed back to El

Dorado. I was afraid I had done something wrong. Don and I returned to Mr. Kilgore's office together. Mr. Small thanked the bank president for his business and asked where the bonds should be sent for safekeeping and payment. Mr. Kilgore instructed us to send the bonds to the First National Bank in Kansas City. The order was confirmed, and we walked out of the bank. When we got to Don's car, I asked why he'd felt he had to come all the way back out to El Dorado, when he could have just told me what to do on the phone. He said, "Wally, I've been in this business for twenty years, and I have never sold this bank a bond."

For the next few years, I was on the road constantly, putting thousands of miles on my Buick. (As soon as I had the money, I bought the Buick from Don, who sold it to me for a low price.) From Wichita, my territory went north to Nebraska, east to Missouri, and south to Oklahoma. There were many weeks when I left home on Monday morning and was gone all week. I stayed at small motels and ate at local cafés and diners in rural Kansas. I worked from first light, driving from town to town, and I called on banks until there was no one else to see. I drove in every kind of weather: snowstorms, ice storms, and blizzards in winter; the shimmering heat of summer; and dust storms so intense that I would have to pull over and wait until they passed. At night, I would fall into bed exhausted and lonely.

When I was in the larger cities, such as Topeka, I met other bond salesmen who told me I'd starve trying to sell securities by driving all over eastern Kansas. I told them I had no choice. This was what my boss wanted me to do, and I'd make the best of it. In reality, meeting with bankers all over the eastern part of the state served me well. I developed personal relationships with many of them and often stopped in to just say hello or buy them lunch. I was never a high-pressure salesman and built relationships that could never have happened with just a phone call. I got a salary, expenses, and commission. I was working hard and doing well.

Lorrie was home with our children, who now included our baby girl, Cathy. Our family wasn't planned, and I teased Lorrie that all I had to do was walk into the room and she'd get pregnant. We still lived in our rented home, which we had fixed up over time, and it was comfortable. Doors continued to open for me, and we began to talk about buying a home. I wanted to provide all the things for my wife and children that I'd never had. Financial security was at the top of the list. I was determined to be a good husband and father and make my family proud.

I could never waste my life, as my parents had, and I would never embarrass and humiliate my family, as my parents had done to me. Everyone who knew my father said he was a talented man. He was a mechanical whiz who could fix anything, and his musical talent was well known. Whatever talent he had got lost in drink. My mother was a pretty woman, people said. I wouldn't know; I hardly ever saw her. What I do know is that she never held or comforted me. My sister and I were invisible to her, and if she cared for us at all, we never knew it.

I became a student of success; I watched and learned everything I could about successful people. If they dressed a certain way, I dressed the same way. I changed how I talked and presented myself. I was observant and began to mimic every behavior of the people who had what I wanted to have. I wanted to become one of them. I regretted the tattoo on my arm—I'd regretted it from the day I'd discovered it after my night on the town while in the coast guard. Now I kept it well hidden with long-sleeved shirts. The tattoo represented the life I wanted to leave behind, not the life I was determined to have.

I always enjoy meeting people and talking to them about what they do for a living. There is always something to learn. One time, I was in a conversation with a father and son who had run a bowling alley in Wichita and were interested in opening their own bowling alley. They asked if I would like to be their partner. I would get 51 percent if I could secure the money. I was able to get a loan from an investment firm in Chicago, and I became a partner in my first business venture. My partners ran the operation, and our AMF bowling alley was successful. I owned half of the business with no cost, no investment, and no obligation. The business would pay off the loan over time. I began to see how I could use other people's money to make money.

As I traveled back and forth from one town to another, I saw that owning my own airplane would make my life easier and allow me call on customers without having to endure the long, boring drives across eastern Kansas. I bought my first airplane, a Piper Tri-Pacer, before I learned to fly. My good friend Bill Fildes thought I was crazy to buy the plane first, but I knew exactly what I wanted to do, and I did it.

I had often gone flying with another friend, Jerry York, who had been in the air force and was a private pilot. He used to rent airplanes from the McConnell Air Force Base Aero Club and take me flying with him. He'd let me fly the plane, and I got a feel for navigation. I could hear him talking on the radio to the tower, and he'd tell me what was happening. I loved flying and was confident that this was something I could do. When I took my flying lessons, the instructor was surprised how quickly I learned, and I soloed in seven hours.

Once I had my pilot's license, I was able to fly to any small town in eastern Kansas that had a landing strip and a bank to call on. My sales increased, as I was able to travel from one location to another more quickly. My long, tedious days on the road were over. I was tired of being away from my family all week. Now I could fly most any place I needed to go and be home in time for dinner. I missed seeing my kids every day and being able to spend time with them. One time, I arrived home to find a fire truck in front of the house. Our son Mikey, who was about three, had locked himself in the bathroom and had turned on the hot water. Steam was coming from under the door, and Lorrie was afraid he would be scalded to death before she could get him out. The firemen rescued Mikey, and he wasn't hurt, but the incident scared Lorrie and me. Having a plane didn't guarantee that I'd be home for every emergency, but at least I could be home more often.

The only close call I had as a pilot happened when my mother and her husband visited us. My stepfather, Ray, wanted me to take him for a ride in my airplane, but my plane was getting a hundred-hour inspection and was not available. I called the airport to see if they had a loaner I could use for a few hours, and they did. It was not a beautiful day to fly, as it was misty and cold, but we got in the airplane and flew around in a forty-mile radius to see the sights in the area around Wichita. When we came back, I got in the pattern and came in for the landing. I put the gear down, and we came in at about eighty miles per hour. When the nose gear hit the runway, the plane veered suddenly to the left, toward an airplane hangar. The nose gear had frozen into a sideways position. I instantly kicked the right rudder pedal, which immediately turned the plane to the right and back onto the runway. It was a close call and scared us both. I found out later that the loaner was there to have its shimmy damper fixed, which had caused the frozen nose gear, and they shouldn't have rented it out at all. I never rented another airplane. I knew my own plane, and if there was a problem, I would know not to fly it until the problem was fixed.

My mother did not visit often and came only when she needed something. This time was no different. Both she and her husband were down and out, with no jobs and no place to go. Lorrie and I let them stay with us, but I didn't trust either of them, so I rented them a furnished apartment, paid their utilities, and helped them move in. I called a friend who owned a large investment-banking firm to ask if he would interview my stepfather for any job he was capable of doing. My friend agreed, and I told Ray to put on a suit and tie for the interview. When he got back, I asked how it had gone. "It didn't go too well," he said.

"Well, what happened?" I asked.

"They offered me less money than you are making, so I didn't take the job," he replied.

"You know, I've been at this awhile," I said. I just shook my head. Why had I even tried to help? A week later, I called their apartment, but there was no answer. After several attempts, I went to the apartment to check on them, but they were gone.

After a couple of days, I got a phone call from Grant Davis, a car dealer in town, who had sold me several cars. "How did your folks like their new car?" he asked.

"What car?" I answered, fearing the worst.

"Your parents came in and said you told them to pick out a car and that you'd pay for it. They drove off in a new Pontiac."

"Well, I never told them they could buy a car, but I'll pay for it," I told him.

I found out a few days later that they had been drinking and wrecked the car on the way to Kansas. Grant would not allow me to pay for the car, as he said the dealership had insurance to cover stolen cars. I told him how sorry I was this had happened. I was embarrassed and depressed. Nothing would ever change with my parents, no matter how hard I tried. I knew I was trying to buy my mother's love, and I sadly still wanted her to be proud of me. My mother never called to apologize for what happened, and I didn't hear from her again for years.

We were in Wichita for several years before we decided to buy a home in Arkansas City, Kansas. Arkansas City—or Ark City, as it is often called—was a town built on the confluence of the Arkansas and Walnut Rivers. Ark City had a population of about thirteen thousand people at the time and was a great small town, with breathtaking natural beauty. Lorrie and I decided that this would be a wonderful place to raise our family and were excited to buy a two-story brick home called the Patterson House in the nicest neighborhood in Arkansas City. Lorrie and I were right about our decision to move. We loved our new home and quickly became acquainted with all the families in our neighborhood. I continued to do well in the investment business and paid cash for a brand-new Cadillac that I proudly parked in front of our home.

Several years passed, and I decided to form my own company, Noel and Company, to use for my investment business and for other side businesses. Don Small and I parted on good terms and remained close friends. I got my broker-and-dealer license in Oklahoma, which allowed me to expand my investment business outside the state. Over time, I developed many loyal customers in the banking business who would hand me the portfolios of their bond holdings to make the decision about which securities they should buy and sell. I discovered that bank accountants disliked the paperwork involved with premium and discount bonds, so I developed par (face-value) bond packages using both premium and discount bonds, which balanced each other, thereby eliminating the paperwork. My customers loved that idea, and my par bond packages became my biggest seller. I always listened carefully to what my customers were telling me. I asked a lot of questions and tried to figure out a way to give them what they wanted. Finding out what the customer needs and then delivering that product to them makes selling easy.

Before long, I bought a Brunswick bowling alley and the Memorial Lawn Cemetery in Arkansas City. The cemetery was a deal I couldn't pass up. I learned the owners wanted to sell the cemetery, so I decided to look into it. I asked to see the books. After years of looking at numbers in the investment business, I was able to quickly assess the situation. I saw there was $40,000 in a perpetual fund to maintain the cemetery and began to ask questions. I found out that if I secured the fund with a deed of trust on commercial land, I would be able to use the fund for the cemetery any way I pleased. I owned the land next to the bowling alley, so I got a deed of trust and paid for the cemetery with the money in the perpetual fund. I then used the income from sales of cemetery plots to maintain and improve the property. Being creative with financing allowed me to buy this business without using any capital. The owner was so mad when he found out, because he had not thought of it first.

Thinking outside the box was something I was always able to do. I didn't try; it just seemed obvious to me. Why hadn't someone else already thought of this? I learned you don't need to beat around the bush or think something to death—just get to it, or someone else will.

I was always busy with business, but my life revolved around my family. There are times when things happen that remind you just how precious life is. The Bollinger family lived in our neighborhood. They had three sons in the same age range as our two boys, Larry and Michael. We enjoyed many happy times together with their family, sharing meals, picnics, and barbecues together. Little John, their youngest boy, had cystic fibrosis, a hereditary disease that was eating away at his young life. By the time we met the Bollingers, Little John was fragile and needed oxygen to keep him alive. We kept an oxygen tent in our home for him so that he could come over and watch the boys play and live as normal a life as possible. Little John never complained of his discomfort; he managed his pain with a smile on his face.

The time came when he could no longer stay, and he was hospitalized. We visited as often as we could. I will never forget the last time we visited him in the hospital. My sons loved to wear cowboy boots, and Little John thought the boots were great. We bought Little John a pair of cowboy boots, and when we went to visit him that night, I placed them on the table next to his bed, where he could see them. He opened his eyes, and although he was exhausted, when he saw those boots, his smile was enough to light up a room. I encouraged him that he would be able to wear them soon. He was so happy. My heart broke for Little John. I learned how tough he was and how much love he had for all of us. I'm sure he hid much of his pain so as not to sadden his family or mine. I looked into his eyes, and I could see that the light of life was nearly out. The next day, I got a phone call that he had died in the night. He never got to try on his cowboy boots. My heart broke. I can still see his smile in my mind and hear his voice; I honor the time we had with him.

Later that day, my wife and I realized the financial stress the Bollinger family was under. After we discussed what we could do, there was no question. I had a cemetery and the money to bury him. His family and I picked out the headstone, and it was done. I believe my buying that cemetery was fate. I loved that little boy, and being able to help the family also helped me in those sad days. One thing I am sure of: love never goes away; he is with me still. Losing Little John Bollinger taught me that life is precious and often taken for granted. I vowed I would live each day with meaning and purpose.

Lorrie and I stayed close to the family, but my business kept me on the go. My wife and kids were happy, my businesses were doing well, and I was confident our future was secure. I felt on top of the world. It is amazing how things can change in a day, and I now understand you have to be ready. One day, to my surprise, I received a summons that I had been called in on a lawsuit. I had two bowling alleys: an AMF bowling alley in Wichita and a Brunswick bowling alley in Arkansas City. AMF and Brunswick compete nationally in the manufacture of electronic and automated equipment used in the bowling industry. AMF alleged that Brunswick had advertised certain automatic devices in a false and deceptive manner. Brunswick responded with counterclaims regarding advertisements for AMF's pin spotters, bowling pins, and automatic scorers. These two companies were national giants, but I was just a small businessman who happened to have the bad luck of owning one of each. Because of the lawsuit, I was caught in the middle and was unable to continue operating my businesses. I couldn't sell either business because of the active lawsuit. After consulting with my attorney, he advised me to file bankruptcy. He said this would cost more to fight than it was worth. I was devastated. Everything I had worked for up to this point was about to vanish.

Chapter 5

While I knew what my attorney had said was probably true, I looked at the situation from every angle before I finally agreed that starting over was my only choice. Filing bankruptcy was against all I believed. My word was my bond, and a handshake was as good as a contract. I promised myself that in spite of the bankruptcy, I would eventually pay all my creditors what I owed them and restore my good name. Lorrie and I reluctantly sold our beautiful home and moved into a smaller house across town. I lost all three businesses: two bowling alleys and the cemetery. The only asset I had left was myself; there was no one to dig us out of this hole but me. However, I believe that sometimes we cannot deny fate and that somehow we were meant to own that cemetery when it was needed for our friends.

After the bankruptcy, I had to regroup, stiffen my back, and start my business career over. Luckily, I had a family who stood by me and never complained. I thought I had better stick with investment banking. There was a fairly new instrument to use that enabled states, cities, and counties to issue industrial revenue bonds to entice industries to move to their area. I became interested and began selling them along with the other securities I typically sold. I always tried to get ahead by being in front of everyone else, and I could see a lot of potential in selling this type of bond.

Industrial revenue bonds are an excellent tool to help areas create jobs, but few people in the industry were using them. Investment bankers are conservative by nature and generally stick to the status quo. The bonds allowed states, counties, and cities to lend their names to these securities at favorable interest rates, but the municipality was not liable for them. The interest on this type of security is tax exempt to purchasers, which is an enticement for the industry to buy them. I started scouting out industries that would be interested in relocating to more-advantageous states, counties, or cities to do business. Most of the companies didn't realize that industrial revenue bonds existed. I started looking at cities and states that had higher taxes, higher costs of living, labor unions, and other factors that affected their costs of doing business. I went to those areas to find large companies and encourage them to go to a municipality that could issue the bonds and move their company to a more favorable location. After going to the company and seeing their needs, I would scout cities, counties, or states that could meet their requirements. In time, buying and selling this type of security became a large part of my investment business.

After several years of hard work, my business started to flourish, and I was able to recuperate from my bankruptcy. I felt one of my first responsibilities was to pay off my creditors, even though I did not legally have to do so. I eventually paid back $46,000 to cover my past debts and recover my good name. My banker, Bob Docking, helped me through these times by not pressuring me on my loans. Lorrie and I found a larger, more comfortable home and bought it. The new home also had enough room for me to have an office, which allowed me to run my business out of our home. This rebirth of our lives was a welcome relief for us all; we felt like a new dawn was shining. As time moved on, I began to have more confidence in myself. Before long, we joined both the Arkansas City Country Club and the Lancer's Club in Wichita to use for social and business purposes.

I was not the same man I used to be. My work took me around the country, and I was in contact daily with the top leaders of cities, states, and industry. I was no longer the small-town kid trying to find his way; I was a respected businessman. Still embarrassed by my tattoo, I tried to have it removed, but it was too deep for a laser to erase, so I kept it well hidden. I encouraged Lorrie to change with me and learn how successful people lived. I enjoyed buying my wife beautiful clothes, as she didn't seem to have the desire to do so. As our social circles changed and grew, I began to get attention from women, which I had not gotten before. This was a new problem I had to deal with. Lorrie knew other women were flirting with me and became jealous. I had been too busy working and trying to keep our heads above water to have time for a social life. Now we were entering social circles we'd never had access to before. I'll admit I was flattered by the attention, but I enjoyed being successful even more. I think Lorrie sensed that success had changed me and feared we were growing apart well before I knew there were problems ahead.

One of my first business principles was to always treat people fairly, and many of my customers became close friends. I learned that the art of making a deal is to always try to find a way in which everyone wins.

Selling industrial revenue bonds gave me many such opportunities. If I could entice a company to move to a more favorable location for its business, the municipality gained a new industry, the company increased its revenue, and I made money making the deal. Win, win, win. It always seemed an obvious business strategy to me.

Noel and Company was doing well with the help of many business associates who provided me with contacts. I brought a number of businesses and plants to Arkansas City and Oklahoma using industrial revenue bonds, including Ziegler Helicopter, Sequaria Mills Rug Company, and a poultry processing plant. These companies brought thousands of jobs to the local areas. *There were no bounds for my ambition, and each successful deal fueled my desire to find and close the next one. My confidence grew with the knowledge that people believed in my abilities as a businessman.*

I met a lot of politicians during this time. Senator Raymond Horn respected my involvement in the growth of Oklahoma and mentioned that he had a friend who could probably use my help. Of course I was willing, and he introduced me to one of his ranching neighbors, Carl Mercer. Mr. Mercer owned Hollywood Deeptone Manufacturing, a huge muffler plant that served much of the automobile industry. He invited my wife and me out to California to see his operation and visit about business. I explained industrial revenue bonds to him, and he was interested because he was about to go broke with the high wages, overhead, and property taxes in California. I convinced him that he could cut his costs dramatically by moving his plant to Harmony, Oklahoma, Senator Horn's district. After much thought, he decided it would benefit his company to move to Oklahoma. With an airport close to the new site and a horse ranch he owned, also in Oklahoma, it was a perfect fit.

The business became considerably more profitable after the move, and Carl was delighted. Our friendship grew, and Carl often invited Lorrie and me to his ranch for the weekend. We all enjoyed riding horses, and Carl owned a stable full of prize-winning quarter horses. Carl indicated that the bond issue could have saved his company, and in appreciation, he presented me with Kennedy Bars, a beautiful quarter horse sired by the world-famous quarter horse Three Bars. Carl also gave my wife a big dun horse to take home. We boarded our horses on a ranch in Ark City, and my interest in quarter horses began. I started to go to horse auctions and purchased several more. The beauty of these animals was amazing, and I loved having them.

While standing outside of our home one day, I noticed that the ranch across the road was for sale. It was an eighty-acre ranch in a perfect location. I wanted a place to raise my quarter horses, and I quickly set my mind to buy the property. I knew that this would be a good investment and would be a wonderful thing for my boys to be involved in. We bought the ranch and immediately began making improvements. We started construction on a barn for hay and grain storage and added stalls and some runs for the horses.

My boys loved being cowboys. We now had a full horse-training facility with starting gates, a racetrack, and a hot walker to cool the horses down after workouts. My sons, Larry and Michael, rode bulls and broncs; their love for animals was as natural as my love for them. I was so proud of how seriously they took their responsibilities; they cleaned the barn and stalls and groomed the horses. I wanted my children to be respectful of people and not afraid of hard work. I believed their reputation should precede them. I was proud of my boys. I made sure they had a horse trainer who taught them the ropes of horse breaking and training. They formed bonds of unconditional love for our horses, just as we had bonds of unconditional love for each other. *Watching my boys thrive at the ranch touched me deeply. Their childhood looked nothing like mine, and I was happy I could provide for them.*

One day, as Michael was riding a colt he was training, his right stirrup broke, and the colt sent him flying into the barbed-wire fence. Thank God he had on a leather rough-out vest! The front of the vest was shredded, but it had saved him from serious injury. Michael was a tough kid. He cleaned up and got right back on that horse.

I often think back on all our family outings together. Although my girls didn't enjoy the ranch in the same way my boys did (Sandy was now in high school, and my youngest, Cathy, was too little), they did join us on fishing trips and other adventures. Life was good. I was living everything I had dreamed. I never took my family for granted. Even while spoiling my children, I was sure to instill in them the values of knowing right from wrong, having good ethics, and the importance of a strong character.

What was wrong with my parents? I had no more natural talent than my father; I just made the most of what I had been given. My parents did not give us love or work to instill values in us. They certainly did not lead by example. What they did give me was a certainty that the life they had was one I would never live and that my children would never have to experience the pain of my past.

Chapter 6

I now had business contacts all over the country, and through those contacts, I heard that there was a guy in Arlington, Texas, who wanted to sell half his interest in a Pizza Hut he owned. Everyone in Kansas knew that Pizza Hut was going nuts and was aware of the growing success of the Carney brothers' enterprise. I figured there might be something to learn from their success and decided to pursue this opportunity. Before I could buy the half interest, however, I would need to obtain permission from Pizza Hut. I made an appointment with Frank Carney at his office in Wichita, Kansas.

I entered Mr. Carney's office and introduced myself. Frank was a fine-looking young man in his late twenties or early thirties, with dark hair and a friendly smile. We immediately hit it off. I told him of my desire to buy into the Pizza Hut in Arlington and asked to see the books. Frank produced the documents, and when I scanned the books and saw what the store was doing each month, I had all the information I needed. I wanted in. The return on investment was phenomenal. Frank gave his permission, and I left his office certain that this would be a great opportunity. I immediately mailed a check for $20,000 to the store owner in Arlington and completed the deal. I never laid eyes on the place before I bought it. Three weeks later, my first check from Arlington came in the mail. It was for $1,000. Each month, succeeding checks arrived with my share of the profits, anywhere from $1,000 to $1,500. At this rate, my initial investment would be paid off in less than two years.

I think this entry into the franchise industry was enlightening and a new way of thinking about business. My interest in the Arlington Pizza Hut taught me that a business could produce income for us while leaving me free to pursue the investment banking business. When I realized I didn't have to be full-time hands-on to make something work, it was an awakening—and a long way from my days on the assembly line. Making money while I slept! That was a concept I could never have dreamed existed, but here it was before me.

I could see that expanding the number of Pizza Hut stores I owned was a golden opportunity. I let others in the industry know that I was interested in buying additional stores. Franchise owners are like a small community; when word goes out on the wire, everyone knows in short order. I soon got a call from a franchisee in Corpus Christi, Texas, who owned five Pizza Huts that he wanted to sell along with the rights to a large development area. I was taking my family to the World's Fair in San Antonio, and I told him I'd stop on my way there.

The owner of the franchise wanted to sell his five Pizza Huts, as none of them were doing well, and all were losing money. When he took us to see the stores, and I saw what was going on, I knew why he was losing money. It wasn't rocket science; the places were dirty, and the employees were not trained. College kids were in the restaurants with no shoes or shirts, playing dominos and drinking beer. Grass was growing through the cracks in the parking lots, where young adults were smoking pot. The picture was clear to me, so I put that all in my mind and went on to the World's Fair with my family.

After returning from our vacation, I went back to Corpus Christi to talk to this gentleman and asked what he wanted for his Pizza Huts. "Five hundred thousand dollars," he said.

"No," I replied. "I'm not interested in that number." We negotiated some; I didn't want to insult him with all I thought had to be done. Then I said, "I'll tell you what I'll do. I'll give you three hundred thousand for the stores and the development area, paying you fifty thousand a year over six years."

He immediately agreed that we had a deal; we drew up the contract, and I gave him a check for $50,000. I was elated; this was a kick-ass deal, and I knew it. I was confident I could bring these stores around and make them profitable, and when I did, they would pay for themselves and then some. Each store had to make only $10,000 a year in profit to pay the purchase price; everything above and beyond that was gravy.

I hired my good friend from Wichita, Jerry York, to be the area manager. We went to Corpus Christi and closed all five Pizza Huts for renovation. We told the employees that when we were ready to reopen, they could reapply for their old jobs, and if we hired them, we'd supply training. Most employees took us up on the offer and came back. The renovations were not extensive, as all the restaurant equipment was in great shape. We redid the interiors, cleaned them up, touched up the paint inside and out, repaved the parking lots, and hired an off-duty police officer to keep transients out of the parking lots. I then put a sign on the front door that said, "No shoes, No shirt, No entry!" I thought, *If you're going to come in here and drink beer, you're going to have it with a pizza—and your clothes on!* At first, Pizza Hut was not happy with my decision to close the stores and put up the sign, but they changed their minds when they saw that in less than a year, all five of the stores were profitable.

When I bought the five stores in Corpus Christi, I needed to have my businesses insured. I met with an insurance salesman who suggested I get business-interruption insurance since Corpus Christi is located on the Gulf Coast. I had never owned property on a coast before, but I could clearly remember some wicked storms on the Great Lakes while in the coast guard, so I said, "What the heck? Let's do it." The insurance salesman did me a huge favor that day! I never would have thought to ask for business-interruption insurance on my own, as I didn't even know it existed. But as fate would have it, a couple of years later, when the businesses were all doing well, disaster struck. On August 3, 1970, Hurricane Cecilia, one of the most destructive hurricanes ever to hit the Texas coast, roared into Corpus Christi. In less than a half hour, extreme winds with microbursts of 160 miles per hour raked through the business and residential areas of Corpus Christi, leaving eleven dead and incredible damage in its wake. The storm wiped out my five stores!

My insurance policy with the special rider saved the day. Not only did I get five brand-new stores fully furnished with new restaurant equipment, but the policy also paid our payroll and gave us our monthly gross revenue during the months we were closed. We didn't miss a beat, and I never owned another store without buying business-interruption insurance, the best safety net money can buy.

There is risk in all business, but minimizing my risk was always forefront in my mind. Sure, I had money to invest, but I had also experienced losing it all through no fault of my own. Who can predict when a hurricane might strike and how much damage it will do? Earthquakes? Fires? I had crawled out of one hole and didn't want to ever do it again. Sometimes you have to learn the hard way. This time, I came out on top.

Chapter 7

My business holdings continued to expand as I learned to reinvest profits for growth. I bought the franchise rights to three towns: Arkansas City, Wellington, and Winfield, Kansas. This was a nice grouping of restaurants within miles of each other and close to home. At the same time, I was expanding the number of Pizza Huts I owned in my territory in Texas. I went to the cities and counties in that area and got acquainted with bankers and other people who knew the towns and could guide me. I traveled those cities myself and found potential locations, mapped them, did all the demographics, researched local union problems, and found out if road construction was planned in those areas. I did my homework before I invested any money in a location, having learned that time spent up front saves time and money in the long run. A good location is essential for a restaurant's success. If a restaurant is hard to find or inconveniently located, customers will go to its competitors to eat. I continuously reinvested profits from existing stores into opening new stores because I strongly believed that investing in our future would pay off in the long run.

One day, I received a phone call from a gentleman who had a Pizza Hut territory in Louisiana and offered to sell it to me for eleven thousand dollars. I immediately said I'd buy it. I was feeling pretty good about this transaction. The next day, I received a call from another man in Louisiana, inquiring about the territory I had just bought. He said he was interested in that area. I explained I had just bought it. He then offered me almost five times more than I'd paid for the territory. Again, I did not hesitate in saying yes. How lucky that in one day, I bought a territory in Louisiana for eleven thousand dollars and sold it the next day for a nice profit before I had even mailed my check. That transaction certainly made my day! What a great country!

I felt grateful that Lorrie was such a good mother and homemaker, which gave me time to put my business deals together. I was away from home regularly, working both my investment business and my Pizza Hut franchises. One door opened, and then another door would open. I was not just becoming financially secure; I was learning and living a life I had not even dreamed about when I'd started Noel and Company.

It was as if life smiled on me, and I did not think I could have a bad day until my dear friend Bill Fildes got me involved in purchasing a lease to drill a gas well. Sure enough, the well hit, and we thought we had made a great investment. However, Bill had not checked to make sure there were distribution lines for the well, and there were none, making the well worthless. We had been scammed. I quickly learned I had to stay on top of any deals Bill brought my way. We were both disappointed and lost several thousand dollars each on this deal, but we gained knowledge about what not to do.

It is easy to get complacent when you have made many deals that have worked out well. It is also easy to let down your guard when a good friend is excited about making a deal and wants you to be part of it. I always looked at a deal closely before I signed on, but not that time. I realized I would have to take the time to do my own research before I signed on the dotted line. Bad deals don't just happen; you allow them to happen—and I was determined to not make the same mistake twice.

Bill owned a car dealership and commercial buildings on the east side of the main street in Arkansas City. When I saw five commercial buildings on the west side of the street were for sale, I decided to look into it. All five buildings were fully rented with longtime tenants, and when I worked the numbers, I knew that this was a good deal. I went to see my friend Bob Docking at the Union State Bank, and he did not hesitate to give me a loan to buy these properties. With the buildings fully rented, I could pay off the loan in five years. Like the Pizza Huts I owned, I'd let the businesses pay the loans and, over time, let them pay for themselves. Years later, I'd sell the buildings for four to five times what I'd paid for them. That's the kind of deal I like!

My family and I loved our ranch in Arkansas City, so I decided to buy another ranch as an investment outside of Winfield, Kansas. My friend Bill bought a ranch right across the street. As you can see, we enjoyed each other's company! Bill, always looking out for me, noticed that there was a beehive in one of the walls of my ranch house. He also had some bee issues at his place. He decided to smoke the bees out of my ranch. Bill got a hot power smoker to drive the bees out and get the honey. The smoker got so hot that it caught my house on fire! It just so happened that that day, I had decided to ride out to the ranch, and as I drove up the road, I saw a fire truck, Bill, and the smoldering debris of my burned-down ranch house. Bill was distraught, crushed, and embarrassed that he had burned down my place, not his. He had a good heart, and there was no way I could be angry with him. After all, the place was insured, and the house could be rebuilt. My friendship with Bill remained strong, and we laughed about this for years to come—I still do!

Chapter 8

My family and I loved the ranch business and always enjoyed our time on our ranches. My travels with Noel and Company were now taking me all over the country. Bill Fildes and I were on a business trip in Sedan, Kansas, when he introduced me to Sheriff George Wayman, and through the sheriff, I met a rancher named E. C. Mullendore.

E. C. Mullendore was a young man in his thirties who ran his family's ranch in Osage County, Oklahoma. E. C.'s grandfather, Erd, who staked the original claim in the Oklahoma Land Rush, started the Cross Bell Ranch. Erd expanded the ranch by buying nearby properties, as did his son, Gene Mullendore, E. C.'s father. By the time I met E. C., this was not just a ranch; it was a ranching empire covering thousands and thousands of acres. I had never seen such a lifestyle as the Mullendores lived. You could compare it to the television program *Dallas*.

E. C. had a great personality, and we hit it off well. We had some great times together, roaming all over the ranch, checking the cattle and horses. I remember when E. C. put metal shields on the undercarriages of his cars so that we could ride over the rough terrain and not destroy the undercarriages. We were men acting like boys, chasing herds of buffalo while doing our best not to get thrown out of the car. E. C. even gave me a portable phone, which was about the size of a brick and weighed the about the same; it had a short range, but we had fun with them.

My wife and I attended some of the most wonderful parties at the Cross Bell Ranch, and E. C. and his wife became our close friends. I hadn't known E. C. for long before I recognized that E. C. was a great guy, but I saw that his dad, Gene Mullendore, put a lot of pressure on him. There was no doubt that Gene Mullendore was the baron of the Mullendore ranching empire, and I didn't think E. C. was as confident as I thought he should be. E. C. was a nice guy, maybe too nice, compared to his iron-willed, intimidating father, and many people took advantage of him.

Gene Mullendore directed the business decisions of the family, and enlarging the empire was always paramount. Everyone in the area was aware that the Mullendores were land hungry and knew they would pay inflated prices to get more land. Consequently, while the empire continued to grow in size, profits did not follow. Those in the area called E. C.'s wife, Linda, the Jackie Kennedy of Osage County, and she spent money as if the supply were endless. For years, I thought it was! The sprawling ranch, beautiful homes, cars, racehorses, and immense herds of cattle convinced me that this family was richer than I could ever imagine.

Because E. C. and I were close friends, he shared with me that he admired my independence and business savvy. He longed to have a part in a business that he could control, and I agreed to sell him a small percentage in a few of the Pizza Huts I owned. E. C. and I shared an office in Tulsa, and we had a great time working together. We jointly bought a Cessna 310 twin-engine airplane, which was more suitable for longer trips and night flying. I then hired a pilot so that I could concentrate on expanding my territories. Working with E. C. was always a kick, and I thoroughly enjoyed his company whatever we did together.

I helped E. C. obtain a $90,000 loan at my bank for his ranching operations. I never thought anything of it; I assumed that the ranch got loans and repaid them as a normal cycle of their business. I was wrong. The Mullendore ranching empire was deeply in debt, and E. C. was taking loans to cover other loans, eventually getting money from increasingly shady characters. He never let on to me that he was in serious financial trouble. As far as I was concerned, he was continuing to live the good life.

One day, I was at home in Arkansas City, when I received a phone call that E. C. had been murdered—shot in cold blood in his home on the ranch. I was stunned! *Murdered?* Fear entered my mind knowing that someone close to me was murdered, not dead of natural causes. The murder was up front in everyone's conversation. It was an uneasy time for anyone who associated with the Mullendores. The FBI visited me at my home with what seemed like a hundred questions. I was as candid as candid could be.

The investigation continued for years, with different theories put forward. Everyone who knew E. C. and the family had his or her own ideas. The murder was a Mafia hit when E. C. couldn't pay on his loans and refused to sign over the ranch. It was an inside job done by someone who wanted E. C. out of the picture. Law officials suspected the ranch hand and bodyguard, who was in the home and was the first to find E. C. dead, because of his past criminal record. A double-indemnity life insurance policy for millions of dollars had just been purchased on E. C.'s life, so he had been murdered for the insurance money. Theories abounded; the family had made plenty of enemies over the years, but not E. C. He was a kind, generous man who had gotten in over his head. We'll never know; his murder has never been solved.

The family held the funeral procession at the ranch, with many people in attendance. There was a riderless horse with E. C.'s boots backward in the stirrups, much like at President Kennedy's funeral. Before they closed the casket, I saw Gene Mullendore pat his son on the arm and say, "There will never be another son of a bitch like you." The service was held on a high hill on the Cross Bell Ranch. Lorrie and I drove our car in the procession with the family and close friends. E. C. was a young man with a full life ahead of him; I stood on the hill and sobbed like a baby. It was a horrible time in my life.

Sometimes I relive the unforgettable times I had with my dear friend and smile. I learned from E. C.'s death that you must treat each day with respect, as you never know if you will have another. I also learned that no matter how large a fortune someone seems to have, it is not always the case. A business, no matter how large, can get in trouble if the money going out exceeds the money coming in. This was true in the Mullendore case, and it ended in the most tragic way—one I never dreamed possible.

Chapter 9

While in Ark City, Lorrie and I talked about a getaway place, and we decided to buy a cabin on Grand Lake in Oklahoma. It was good for the family to get away together. The kids loved fishing and water-skiing on the lake, and we spent a lot of our free time there. We could take the boat to have dinner and relax at the resort. There was also an airstrip on Monkey Island, so every now and then, we would fly down.

By this time, I was politically connected in both Kansas and Oklahoma. Bob Docking, who was my banker in Ark City, had years earlier become the governor in Kansas. The governor of Oklahoma and I became well acquainted when my company helped underwrite the bonds for both the Kansas and Oklahoma turnpikes. I was also instrumental in relocating numerous industries along the new inland waterway project, which opened the Arkansas River to commercial barging. The Arkansas River was shallow through Oklahoma and Arkansas, and this project artificially widened and deepened the river with locks and dams, allowing products to be shipped down the Arkansas River, which eventually connected to the Mississippi River. I found many companies that needed to be close to waterways to ship their products, including a large poultry processing plant. Clem McSpadden, president pro tempore of the senate of Oklahoma, said I had done more for the state of Oklahoma than their entire development department. He and the governor's offices of both states wrote letters to Secretary Udall in support of my appointment to the position as assistant commissioner of resources and development.

Governor Bartlett invited my family to a party celebrating the opening of the inland waterways. When Vice President Humphrey's aide called our home to borrow my plane to take him down to Oklahoma for the grand opening of the inland waterways, Michael, my son, answered the phone. The caller introduced himself and said he was calling for Vice President Hubert Humphrey. Michael said, "Sure you are!" and hung up the phone. Vice President Humphrey was the guest speaker at the celebration and wanted to use my plane to get there. Lorrie and I had a good laugh that Michael had hung up the phone on a request from the vice president! Every day seemed to be an adventure, and I never felt like I was working. I mean this in the most sincere way: I loved what I did, and I loved my life.

While life seemed to be taking me into the fast lane, I maintained my loyalty to my family. I was being pulled in many directions, but I stayed focused on my goals to always take care of my family first and be the parent I'd never had. I believe that if you love what you are doing, you can have fun and can also prosper.

My friends and other businessmen saw I was a person who could solve problems in business deals they found challenging, and they would call me for advice. I could usually come up with a creative solution that no one had thought of. Thinking outside the box was something I was good at, a result of years of having to make something out of nothing. Now I was connected to heavy hitters in both business and politics and found that my past experiences gave me both a unique perspective and the ability to get things done, and those qualities were in great demand. Business couldn't have been better.

In between business deals, Bill Fildes and I got a big group of friends together and leased a jet to fly us to Monte Carlo. I must have left the reservations up to Bill, because when he arrived at the Loews Monte Carlo Hotel, the girl at the reservation desk said, "I'm sorry, but there is no reservation for Wally Noel." I explained I was with the group, and I was sure I had a reservation, but she insisted that I did not. I was upset. I looked her straight in the eyes and said, "Lady, have you ever seen a grown man lay on his back on the floor and scream and kick his feet?"

She answered, "Of course not!"

"Well, you'd better get the manager over here, or you are going to see it!" The manager came over, and I explained the problem. He looked at the situation, and I ended up with a room with a bar and a balcony that overlooked the Monte Carlo Yacht Club. Not too shabby!

That evening, we were having a great time, and then Bill met a lady who had a little three-wheel car with a top that lifted off so you could get in. Bill was gone before I knew it. He was gone over night. Evidently, they went back to Italy and partied all night. Several of us went to the casino, and I ended up winning $43,000. I put my winnings in the cage in my account and then went to the disco. The lady manager of the disco said she would like to show me Monte Carlo, but she had to work. I wasn't sure I had heard her correctly and said, "If you didn't have to work, you would show me around?"

"Yes," she answered.

I saw an opportunity. I went to the casino manager and asked him to look at the action I had given the casino and see if he could get the casino manager the night off. He checked the casino cage and said to me, "Mr. Noel, she has the night off!" She and I had a blast. She took me to several parties in luxurious homes on the hills above the city. These people were jet-setters from all over the world, and there I was, partying with them. When we went back to the hotel, the sun was up, and they were washing the streets down with hoses. This was like no other night in my life.

Bill and I decided not to go back with the group but to fly to Paris for a few days instead. When we left Paris, we flew on the Concorde back to New York. What an incredible flight! Flying on the Concorde is an experience that still remains vivid in my mind. The takeoff and landing, the supersonic speed, the unique design of the aircraft, and the incredible service during the flight were unlike anything I had ever experienced. The whole Monte Carlo vacation was beyond what I could ever have dreamed while growing up in Sweet Springs, Missouri!

Back home again, my friend Bill seemed to challenge our friendship because I was the one who was constantly helping him out of tight spots. This time was different. One evening at the ranch, Bill and his son came knocking on the door. He had just overrun the runway and wrecked his plane. Thank goodness neither one was injured. Bill asked me if I would say I had wrecked his plane, because his medical certification had expired. "Billy, I cannot lie and possibly lose my license," I said. Bill understood and somehow was able to get his medical postdated and keep his license and insurance.

Bill and I had partnerships on other investments, one of which I had a bad feeling about and did not trust. We had money invested with an investment firm in New York City. I had a gut feeling about this firm, and I had long ago learned to go with my gut. I told Bill we had to go to New York and demand that they give our stock certificates to us. When we got there, I asked to see the account manager. He was not happy that we demanded our certificates, but I didn't care. Bill was silent. I was conscious of the office and staff from the time we walked in the door. I could see an older man sitting at a desk when he suddenly fell off his chair onto the floor. I showed some concern, but no one else did. The account manager did not react but looked at me and said, "Well, he's old anyway."

That was enough for me. I looked at Bill and said, "Let's get out of here!"

The account manager brought out a security guard wearing a police hat and tennis shoes. I laughed and said I didn't want this guy walking me anywhere with $200,000 in stock certificates in the street name (which is the same as cash). Instead, Bill and I took the certificates ourselves to the escrow agent and picked up a certified check. Less than a month later, the firm went bankrupt. If we had not cashed out, we would have lost $200,000. When we returned home, we had a lot to celebrate!

Chapter 10

Lorrie and I decided to take a short vacation to Greeley to visit her uncle and aunt. While visiting, we sat in the backyard, talking to her uncle Roy. He began to tell me about a problem with the farm he had that adjoined the city of Greeley. He'd bought this farm with the expectation of developing it, since the property joined the city limits. He had been negotiating with the city for a while. The city told him they wouldn't approve water taps for his development. Roy was beside himself because without water taps, he just had a farm. Because I was in the investment banking business, which involved working with municipalities on various zoning issues, I told him to let me think about his situation.

After studying the matter, I devised a plan that I thought might fly. Like most deals, both parties must benefit. My plan would accomplish this. I asked the city the following: If Mr. Lundvall would donate enough of his farm for an eighteen-hole golf course, would they zone the rest of his farm residential and furnish him with the water taps for his project? I told them he would also need the city to put in a street to his project. After much thought, the city agreed to this plan. I asked the city to let me handle the bond issue. Roy was elated because now he would have a much better project, as the lots on the golf course would be far more valuable. This was a situation where everybody won.

There are many books written on the art of making a deal. I can save you time. The art of making a deal is quite simple. In a deal, everyone wants something; you just have to figure out what the other side might want. When you figure that out, you've got a deal. Sometimes all you have to do is ask. In other cases, you put yourself in the other person's position and think what offer would get your attention if the roles were reversed. In this case, I thought land donated to enhance the city's public recreation would perk the city's interest. I was right, and the city got an eighteen-hole golf course, Uncle Roy got his development, and my company got the bonds and fees for putting the deal together.

While working on the golf-course issue, Lorrie and I fell back in love with Greeley, Colorado, Lorrie's hometown, where we had lived years earlier. We talked about it at length and decided to move back to Greeley. After searching all over Greeley, we finally found what we wanted: a house known as the Farr House, a beautiful home in a park-like area. We closed on the house and returned to Ark City, Kansas, to prepare for the move to Colorado. The move was going to be difficult, as we had not only our household possessions but also our home, the ranch, and our business properties to deal with. The days of packing up all of our possessions in our car and just heading out of town were long gone. That may have been the way we came to Kansas, but it was not the way we were leaving. We knew we had much to deal with but decided to make the move anyway. Frankly, I was hoping that the move would be good for our marriage and bring us closer together. Like many couples, we seemed to have lost something over the years, and I hoped we could find it again back in Colorado.

Once we had settled in, I started looking for a ranch to buy. After much looking, I found a farm outside of Greeley called the Shark's Tooth Ranch. It had all the things I was looking for, and I bought it. The Shark's Tooth Ranch got its name from the many sharks' teeth found deep in the soil while farming the land. Rumors were that folks believed ocean might have covered that area at some time. (This is true: in prehistoric times, this part of the West was covered by the Western Interior Seaway, which divided the continent into two landmasses. The sea stretched from the Arctic Ocean to the Gulf of Mexico, two thousand miles long and six hundred miles wide.) One thing was for sure: this farm had plenty of water, good soil for crops, and a location perfect for our needs. We wanted to raise cattle and horses. The ranch would be almost self-sufficient, having cropland, grassland, barns, and a nice small home.

We sent our boys, who were both in high school at the time, back to Ark City to get our horses. We had a truck and a four-horse trailer with dually wheels. On the way back, they pulled into a gas station to fill up, and a gentleman in a nice car pulled in behind them. On the hood of his car was a wheel and a tire. Michael and Larry thought this was pretty strange. The man walked over to them and said, "Have you lost something?"

Larry replied, "I don't think so."

They looked around and then saw that one hub and wheel had fallen off the trailer, rolled down the road, and bounced onto the hood of this man's car. The strangest part of this incident was that it didn't do any damage to the man's hood. The boys were still laughing weeks later. There was never a dull moment with my sons.

For the next several years, I continued to run my investment and Pizza Hut businesses from my home in Greeley. Both continued to do well, and although I ventured out into other businesses, my love for ranching was deep in my heart. The golf course that Lorrie's uncle had built was finally near completion, and Lorrie and I built a new home on the golf course I had helped develop. It was a beautiful home with five bedrooms, two garages with space for five cars, a golf cart garage, and a swimming pool. I had given each of my kids a car when they turned sixteen, so we filled the garage space easily.

My son Larry got married shortly after he graduated from high school, and we allowed Larry and his new wife to move into the house at the Shark's Tooth Ranch. Larry wanted to get into ranching in the worst way, and we sent Larry to school at Colorado State University to learn how to artificially inseminate cattle. Larry knew a lot about ranching, having spent so much time working on our ranches in Kansas. I didn't have any worries about leaving Larry in charge; he was as straight as a string.

While at the Denver Stock Show, I saw some magnificent cattle that were the largest I had ever seen. I read the information provided at the stock show and decided to buy a bull and some heifers on the spot. These cattle were Chianina cattle from Italy; a bull thirteen feet long and seven feet tall at the shoulder. They were enormous, and while the price was five times what a domestic bull would cost, I could immediately see the potential in crossbreeding them with the Black Angus cattle I owned. I sent my boys to pick them up and bring the cattle back to our ranch. It turned out that the bull I bought was the first one sold in the United States. I was now in the exotic cattle business, and the Chianina Cattle Association made me their vice president shortly thereafter.

My instinct about this cattle's potential turned out to be correct. The crossbred animals were a third larger than normal Black Angus, producing significantly more meat on the same amount of grass. Additionally, since they were taller, teat infections were reduced. My initial investment in the cattle paid for itself over time, and I never regretted my impulse to buy them.

Instinct? A good guess? Lucky? Being in the right place at the right time is lucky. However, I see this cattle purchase as connecting the dots. My ranching and restaurant experience told me that this animal would produce meat in abundance, more than any cattle in the world. I have always been good with numbers, and something told me that the numbers would work on this deal. Intuition is a gift born of past experiences, and I therefore don't have to think too hard about some of the decisions I make. I sized up these animals and went for it. Sometimes I believe people overthink their next moves and lose both time and money in the process.

While still in Greeley, I had a chance to buy a huge ranch in Wyoming, the Spring Creek Ranch, which covered thirteen thousand deeded acres. The ranch was named for the warm-water creek that ran through it. The creek was a big plus because the cattle had water all winter that didn't freeze over. The barn on the ranch was a huge pole barn that stored tons of hay. We bought a large hay baler that made fifteen-hundred-pound rolls of hay. We'd cut the hay, roll it up, and place the rolls in different meadows so that the cattle would never be without feed.

My foreman, a crusty old cowboy, and I noticed there were cows on a section of our ranch that weren't ours. We had a neighbor who would sneak his cattle to graze on our ranch when he knew our cattle were on another section of the ranch. One day, my foreman and I rode over to his ranch to talk to him about this problem. He said he was sorry his cattle had gotten out and onto our land. Before I could respond, my foreman said back to him, "You sure have got some smart cows, because they are bringing their own salt blocks with them." The look on his face said it all. That ended that problem!

Chapter 11

At this stage of life, I had everything a man could want: a fine home, a great lifestyle, and wonderful kids—but I had one serious problem. I was no longer happy in my marriage. While I continued to love and support my family, I often found it hard to return home. I was not blind to what was going on in my marriage. Lorrie and I had problems, but I kept trying to pretend that nothing was wrong. There was not one specific thing that happened between us, but I had changed in the twenty-plus years we had been together, and I was ready to enjoy everything that life had to offer. Lorrie had also changed but in a different direction. It seemed when we were out at dinner parties, if a woman smiled at me, Lorrie would ask if something was going on with her. No matter how much I would deny it, she didn't believe me. Some of these people were wives of close friends. I was sorry that she thought I would ever cross that line. I found myself depressed, often apologizing for things I was not guilty of. I think it was obvious to us both that we were drifting apart.

Sometime after we returned to Greeley, Lorrie became highly involved in religion, and her religious life was her priority. While I respected her choice, it was not mine, and our life together was a strain for us both. Eventually, I did stray, but I hated that I did. After twenty-one years of marriage, I made the decision to ask for a separation. It was the hardest decision I ever made, and although I can make business decisions in the moment, I struggled for a long time before I knew I had to leave. It was awful! I knew that Lorrie had supported me in everything I had done so far, and when I left, I ensured that she would be well taken care of for the rest of her life. In our agreement, I gave Lorrie most of our liquid assets. In addition to our home, I provided her with lifetime health and dental insurance and a monthly income. I agreed to accept full maintenance of the children, and I took full responsibility for any debts that were outstanding. I did everything I could to protect Lorrie's future, as I should have. I am not sure I ever thought we would actually get back together, but when I left home, a legal separation was all either one of us was willing to do. That separation lasted seven years.

When I moved out of our home, I decided to start my new life in Fort Collins, Colorado, a beautiful community just thirty-two miles northwest of Greeley. I felt as guilty as hell when I left and was sad that our marriage had not worked out. It had been a tough life for us both when we'd started out, and Lorrie had never complained. She had been a good wife and a good mother to our children, but there was no longer any way for us to move forward together and be happy. Ironically, while carrying the burden of guilt and sadness, I also felt a freedom I'd never had before. I had been tied up all my life with responsibilities and could never make decisions just for me. I'd focused my every step on creating a life for my family that I had not enjoyed as a child. My children were now almost grown, I loved what I did for a living, and my social and businesses skills were at a peak. I was a man in a hurry to find out what else life had to offer, and I was determined to find it.

The first thing I needed to do was find a place to live. I enlisted the help of a Realtor and began driving all around Fort Collins looking for a home. We were over by the Fort Collins Country Club when I saw a house sitting on top of a hill with a big, circular drive, and I said, "Well, there's the house I want."

"It's not for sale," he said.

"How do you know that?" I asked. The Realtor looked at his book, told me the house wasn't listed in the multiple listings, and pointed out that there wasn't a For Sale sign. "Well," I said, "that doesn't mean it's not for sale." I didn't have a clue but thought if I knocked at the door and asked, the worst the owners could tell me was no, and I'd say, "Okay," and leave.

I rang the doorbell, and a nice man answered the door. He told me the house was not his, but he ran a school for handicapped children there and had heard talk that the owners might not want to have the school much longer. He didn't know if they would sell the house, but he said he could ask the owners if they were interested. I had horses I wanted to bring from Greeley, and the house was on eight acres. I thought about how great it would be if I could get this house. I had a pretty good idea what property was worth in town, so I said, "I'll tell you what. I'll give you two hundred sixty-five thousand dollars—no contingencies, no inspection, no loan. I'll give you a check, and you give me the deed." He called me back later and said they were going to do it. The house was mine!

There Are No Bounds

I have always been social; I love people and talking to anyone and everyone. I didn't much like being alone and often would go to Old Town in Fort Collins to socialize with friends. I dated some but nothing serious. I was happy to be a single man doing as I pleased. One of the restaurants I used to frequent was the Out of Bounds. While I enjoyed going there, when I went there to eat and watched what was going on, I could see that the place was going to hell in a hand basket. I talked to the two men who owned the place, Ed Massey and Bill James, and found out they wanted to sell, so I bought it and immediately went about turning the restaurant around.

Barb Cain was the manager of the restaurant when I bought the place, and I kept her on. She was a bright, hardworking woman who knew the place was out of control. She told me they were having lots of problems with money, as the waitresses kept coming up short. I told her, "From now on, if the books don't balance, I'll keep the longs, and you and the girls will make up the shorts." That was all I had to say. The stealing stopped.

I also had a bartender who used to sneak his own bottles of liquor in under his coat, sell the customers drinks, and pocket the money. Our liquor inventory didn't come up short, as he was using his own booze, but we weren't making much money in the bar either. In short order, I figured out his scheme and fired him.

Once I got the place turned around, business skyrocketed. The Out of Bounds was the place to be, and there were times it was so packed that people couldn't get into the building. The place was doing so well that when the leases came up, I added an eighty-seat dining room and an outdoor patio, the first in Fort Collins. The restaurant had five dining rooms, three fireplaces, and gorgeous fixtures from England. However, I also knew you can put in carpets two feet thick, but you are not going to fool people very long if you don't have good, happy employees and great food. We did.

When I built the patio at the Out of Bounds, the patio floor was concrete, and we put up a three-foot stone wall around the patio. As soon as the work was completed, the fire marshal came by and told me I'd have to put in a fire escape. "Are you kidding me?" I said. "You could throw a Molotov cocktail on this patio, and there is nothing to burn." Not impressed with my logic, he told me I'd have to put in a fire gate with a kick plate. So I did. Next came liquor control, who told me I couldn't have a gate open to the street without a padlock on it. "Why?" I asked. "If they wanted to take their drink on the street, why wouldn't they just step over the wall?"

"You have to have a padlock with a key; it's city code," he said.

"What do I do with the key in case of a fire?" I asked.

"Give it to the bartender, and they can get the key from him," he replied.

Now I was mad. "Okay, so here's the plan: if there is a fire, the people are going to go inside, get the key from the bartender, and unlock the gate instead of just stepping over the wall?" I said sarcastically. That pissed him off, but I knew we had to do as he said.

Sometimes when building, expanding, or renovating a business, you run into code issues or other bureaucratic nonsense. It would be laughable if it weren't so aggravating and expensive. Common sense is not in the code book, so you just do what they say and move on. I did get the last laugh, however, but that came later.

Roy Noel, my father

Edith Noel, my mother

Wally and sister Geraldine

Wally and Geraldine

Grandparents Alfred and Mary Noel

Grandparents home in Sweet Springs, Missouri, pop.1,000

USCGC Mackinaw

Cutter Mackinaw breaking ice

Boot Camp at 17, Cape May, New Jersey

Wally US AirForce

Wally with son Larry 1955

Children Cathy, Michael, and Larry

Larry Noel

Michael Noel

Cathy Noel

E.C. Mullendore

June 5, 1967

The Honorable Joseph Califano
White House
Washington, D. C.

Dear Joe:

Governor Bob Docking of Kansas and I are among the close friends of Wallace R. Noel of Arkansas City, Kansas, (home of the Governor) who are recommending him for a position as Assistant Commissioner of Resources and Development.

Tom Corcoran, National Committeeman for Kansas, and Governor Docking have written letters of recommendation for Mr. Noel to Secretary Udall. But we are also anxious that he be given extra special consideration and we would like to ask you if you couldn't please request an appointment sometime next week with Secretary Udall. Mr. Noel will be in Washington then.

This is the matter that we discussed briefly over the phone this morning, and I can well understand your being so busy with International affairs that you asked me to put this in writing.

Mr. Noel will phone you next week when he gets to Washington. We all hope that you have been able to get an appointment.

Best personal regards.

Sincerely,

JOHN D. MONTGOMERY
Director of Highways

JDM:fw

Letter of Recommendation from Director of Highways

June 8, 1967

The Honorable Stewart Udall
Secretary of Interior
Washington, D. C.

Dear Stewart:

It has come to my attention that Wallace R. Noel of Arkansas City, Kansas is considering applying for the position of Assistant Commissioner of Resources and Development. It may seem a bit odd to you that I would hasten to recommend a person other than a native Oklahoman for this position. However, I have had the occasion of working with Mr. Noel in industrial expansion throughout the State of Oklahoma and in my opinion, he has done more for industrial and recreational development for our state than our own Industrial Department has.

You are probably aware of the fact that he was instrumental in the recent campaign of Governor Docking of Kansas, and has worked untiringly on the completion of a turnpike program that will link our two states.

I speak for the Oklahoma State Senate as well as hundreds of Oklahomans in urging you to give his name your most serious consideration.

With warmest personal regards, I am

Sincerely,

CLEM McSPADDEN
2nd Senatorial District
President Pro Tempore

CMc:bf

cc: Wally Noel

Letter of Recommendation from Clem McSpadden

THE VICE PRESIDENT
WASHINGTON, D.C. 20510

January 9, 1969

Dear Mr. Noel:

What more can I say but thanks -- and best wishes for the New Year.

Sincerely,

Hubert H. Humphrey

Mr. Wallace R. Noel
1002 North Third Street
Arkansas City, Kansas 67005

Thank you note from Hubert Humphrey

THUNDERBIRD
THE AMERICAN GRADUATE SCHOOL
OF INTERNATIONAL MANAGEMENT

January 11, 2000

Wally Noel
President and CEO
P. J. Management Inc.
Papa Johns Pizza Franchise
1021 N. Orange Grove Boulevard, Unit 104
Pasadena, CA 91105

Dear Wally:

We would like to thank you for speaking to our students at this year's Winterim (2000) Entrepreneurial CEO/Founder Seminar. The program has continued to grow in reputation due to the efforts of Chief Executive Officers like yourself.

Based on the student's enthusiasm, there is no doubt that they enjoyed your presentation.

Thank you once again for taking the time, effort, and expense to come to Thunderbird. It is appreciated by all concerned.

Yours truly,

Paul

Paul R. Johnson
Distinguished Professor of Global Entrepreneurship
World Business Department

PRJ/pg

15249 N. 59th Ave., Glendale, AZ 85306-6000 USA
Phone: (602) 978-7011 ▼ Fax: (602) 439-5432 ▼ *AACSB Accredited*

Thank you letter from Thunderbird University

Pizza Management Inc.

INTERNATIONAL P.O. DRAWER 65100 • SAN ANTONIO, TEXAS 78265-5100 • 512 829-4111
TELEX 510 600-5726 (PMI US) • FAX 512 829-4981

August 18, 1986

Wallace R. Noel
375 East Horsetooth, Shores 2
Suite 202
Ft. Collins, CO 80525

Dear Mr. Noel

On June 20, 1986 at a special meeting of the stockholders of Pizza Management, Inc., the shareholders ratified a stock dividend equal to 150% of the present shares outstanding. This brings the number of shares you hold to 386,448.

Sincerely,

Jon C. Dennison
Secretary/Treasurer

Stock share confirmation

DELHI GAS PIPELINE CORPORATION

February 23, 1996

Mr. Wally Noel
President
Massimo Management, Inc.
2931 Irving Boulevard, Suite 106
Dallas, TX 75247

Dear Mr. Noel:

I was very pleased to read the article in today's Dallas Morning News regarding Massimo's emergence from bankruptcy.

As an avid follower of the restaurant industry and fan of the original Lovers Lane Massimo da Milano, I was intrigued with the previous article, published several months ago, that announced your association with the company.

I was impressed with your quick response to the problems, particularly with providing ownership opportunities for the employees. It continues to amaze me how many establishments while focusing on growth, lose sight of not only their customer's needs but of other basic business principles.

You have apparently mastered the combination of common sense and creativity which seems to be all too rare in today's business environment.

Dallas appears to be an excellent market for establishments that focus on quality and efficiency and apparently you have put Massimo da Milano back on that track.

Congratulations on your accomplishments, and I wish you and your staff continued success.

Yours very truly,

John E. Bonn
Term Sales

L:\HOME\C.YB\WPD\EB\MASSIMO.LTR
Enclosure

1700 Pacific Avenue
Dallas, Texas 75201
214/954-2000

Massimo Letter

Wally donating Chianina bull to CSU

Robin and Wally's wedding 1980

Wally and daughter Cathy at Out of Bounds

Wally and Robin at Bonner Ranch

Robin and Wally in Mazatalan

Our 65' Carver on Kemah Lake

Wally retired living the good life

Chapter 12

With the Out of Bounds running smoothly, I was able to concentrate on my other businesses, and I was always on the lookout for my next deal. I usually didn't have to look hard, as I was often in the restaurant, talking to customers, many of whom offered me deals I couldn't pass up. I traded the Shark's Tooth Ranch for commercial property in a great location in Fort Collins, which I later developed and sold. I bought a drive-in theater in Loveland called the Pines for $150,000, sat on it for three or four years, and sold it for $500,000. I bought a farm west of town with the intention of getting the property rezoned for housing. Once I got that done, I sold the property to a couple of lawyers who wanted to build a housing development they later called the Ponds. I made several hundred thousand on that deal as well. I wanted to get in and out: make the deal, make money, and get out.

One of the best deals I made during that time was when I bought the building the Out of Bounds was in and bought the rest of the County Square, which encompassed one quarter of a city block. One day, the building's owner, Phyllis Mattingley, and I were sitting around shooting the bull, when she said, "I'm thinking of selling the County Square." I was paying her $5,000 a month in rent and knew the other buildings were fully rented with commercial tenants. I asked her how much she wanted for it, and after I got the number, I went to the bank and asked them how long it would take to amortize a loan for that amount if I paid $5,000 a month. When they told me I'd have the loan paid off in five years, I jumped on it. Now, the $5,000 rent I paid, I paid to myself. The money went in the bank to pay off the loan, and the rent from all the other tenants went into my pocket as "fun money." *I love making deals. It's not all about the money; it's like a game, and it is fun to win. I always found the process fascinating and enjoyed the light-bulb moment when I'd figure out how to get things done. Making money was important, of course, but I didn't chase money; I chased the deal. If you follow your dreams and your heart and use your integrity, the money will follow.*

I found another opportunity while talking with Arturo Torres, who was also a Pizza Hut franchise owner. Arturo was of Cuban descent and fluent in Spanish but had had no luck getting Pizza Huts opened in San Juan, Puerto Rico, one of his territories. He asked if I was interested in developing the territory, and I told him I was. We drew up a contract stating I would own 40 percent of any Pizza Huts I opened in Puerto Rico. I did not have to pay him any franchise fee and, therefore, had nothing to lose.

I flew to San Juan, Puerto Rico, with great anticipation but some nervousness. This was not going to be an easy task. I did not speak Spanish, and doing business in a country while having little knowledge of their culture or laws was going to be a challenge for me. The first thing I did was look for a real-estate company to help me scout locations—someone who knew a lot more than I did about local customs and habits. I met a gentleman who fit what I was looking for. Elliot Eaves was an international broker from England, working for Caribbean Properties Ltd. Elliot and I hit it off, and we immediately began scouting locations. I also hired a driver to take me around and show me the island. One area of San Juan was known as Old San Juan. Going there was like going back in time. There were wonderful, well-preserved old homes, narrow streets, and great restaurants and clubs. I was impressed with this city of 2.5 million people and with how friendly the people were. Even with narrow streets that were hard to navigate, I noticed that there was no horn honking, yelling, or people cutting in and out of traffic.

While working with Elliot, he and his girlfriend mentioned they knew a lovely woman I should meet named Judy VanHorn. They didn't think she would go on a blind date, but they said they would ask her anyway. Surprisingly, she accepted. We drove to Judy's penthouse to pick her up, and Elliot went to her elevator and brought her to the car. When I saw her, I couldn't believe my eyes! She was a strikingly beautiful woman with blonde hair and brown eyes. Elliot opened the door for her, and when she looked in and saw me, she said, "I am pleasantly surprised."

"Not nearly as much as I am!" I replied.

The four of us went to a fabulous restaurant that also had entertainment. After dinner, we stayed for the band and show. Part of the entertainment was a belly dancer, a pretty woman who danced topless with a large snake around her neck. She came over to our table during her act, put the snake around my neck, and put my face between her breasts. Judy was furious and asked if we could go somewhere else.

I of course said yes, even though I had taken the incident lightly. We went to another restaurant in Old San Juan and continued to party through the evening. Elliot kept advising me not to come on too strong, but I assured him that I knew how to treat a lady. Eventually, Elliot suggested they take me back to my hotel. Judy broke in and said, "Wally isn't going back to the hotel!" I was pleasantly surprised, to say the least.

During the next several weeks, Judy and I became close. Wherever we went, others always noticed Judy. I was proud to have her on my arm. Judy was not only beautiful but also bright and owned her own real-estate company. She helped introduce me to all the fabulous things San Juan had to offer. I guess Judy was also smitten. She mentioned on several occasions that I should think about going to Hollywood to audition for a series or a movie. I thought this was a wonderful compliment, but I knew I already had my hands full in my business career.

Before I went back to Colorado, I put Elliot and Judy on point for what kinds of locations I needed for my Pizza Huts: walk-up trade, some parking, high-density locations, median income for the area, and no long-term leases or profit sharing with the landlord.

When I returned several weeks later, both Judy and Elliot had found some locations, and I got busy. I stayed with Judy, and even though I had a lot of work to do in San Juan, I had to take time out to enjoy some of the culture and sights of the city and surrounding areas. I visited some of their casinos and was in awe of their beauty. I felt as if I were in some kind of mansion with exquisite chandeliers and fine furniture. Judy showed me a well-preserved old fort that dated back to the sixteenth century and had been a fortification for the Spanish Empire. It was one of the most beautiful spots in Puerto Rico. We also went to Ponce, a quaint city on the southern tip of Puerto Rico. It was a beautiful drive from Ponce back to San Juan through the rainforest.

On subsequent trips over the next eighteen months, I was able to open multiple stores, and an attorney I hired, Jaime Pieras Jr., helped me with any legalities. When I hired Jaime, I was unaware that he was the son of the governor of Puerto Rico, but the fact that he was well connected politically didn't hurt his ability to get things done on my behalf. When I came to San Juan, I lived with Judy and became close to her and her two boys. San Juan became my home away from home, and I loved my time there.

One situation that occurred while I was in San Juan was sad but funny at the same time. Some of the impoverished people who lived in small huts on the beach came into town and started spending large sums of money. Evidently, a boat hauling dope and large bundles of cash had sunk offshore. Both the dope and cash washed ashore, and the natives found it. They came into town and started spending like crazy! They bought clothes, appliances, cars, televisions, and many other luxuries. It didn't take long before the authorities found out about the situation and confiscated all the items they were buying. The police also went out to their little shacks and gathered all the cash and dope the people had found on the beaches. Those people were so poor, and it was sad to see them lose their newfound wealth, but it had to be done, of course.

Whenever I see poor people, especially children, my heart aches for them. I've been there! I can understand why these people went on a spending spree. If they had kept quiet and just spent a little at a time, maybe they could have gotten away with it, but the temptation to get all the things they wanted was too strong. I knew they couldn't keep their windfall riches, and the story of their adventure is funny, but their poverty is not.

I still had my Pizza Huts in Corpus Christi, Texas, and since I would be down there checking on my restaurants, I called Judy and invited her to join me. We had a great time during her visit. I took her on a tour of Corpus Christi, Padre Island, the beaches, and, of course, my Pizza Huts. More than a few times, I thought about making our relationship permanent. However, I had just gotten out of a twenty-one-year marriage and raising four children. Judy's two young boys were great kids, but I wasn't ready to be tied down again and raise another family. I decided to give it more time. Judy and I saw each other for several more months whenever I went back to San Juan. However, eventually, Judy got tired of waiting for me to make a commitment, and after an argument, she packed my bags, and we parted.

When I came back to Fort Collins, a man who wanted to buy my house on Terry Lake approached me. I wasn't too interested in selling, but I was willing to hear what he might offer. What he eventually offered for the house did interest me. He had a large commercial piece of property next to a Cadillac dealership on College Avenue and a beautiful townhome in Parkwood that he wanted to trade for my property. I was single and could live comfortably in the townhome, and the commercial property was a corner lot in a perfect location for business development. A trade has all kinds of advantages. Since no money exchanges hands, there are no taxes to be paid. Whenever I spot a deal too good to pass up, I go for it. Even though I had enjoyed my home, it was not worth holding on to, as an offer like this would not happen again. The art of the deal is not just knowing when to get in but also knowing when to get out. On the commercial property, I eventually made three times the amount of money the house was worth, and I also still had the townhome to live in and eventually sell.

About this time, several ranchers who were interested in buying my Spring Creek Ranch in Wyoming contacted me. The ranch was running five hundred head of cattle at that point and was doing well. I could have kept the ranch indefinitely, but like so many other deals, the time to sell is when you have a buyer, and I'd never intended to be in the ranching business for the long haul. Buy, sell, trade, and increase my bottom line—that was the business I was in. The offer would pay off the loan to the ranch and give me a substantial profit, and I took it. Before I sold the ranch, I donated one of the Italian Chianina bulls to the CSU Animal Reproduction Laboratory to use in embryo transplants, breeding, and general research.

The Pizza Huts I opened in Puerto Rico were all profitable; some became the highest-grossing stores in the organization. I decided to merge many of my Pizza Huts with Pizza Hut Management Inc., a conglomerate of franchise owners, including Arturo Torres, who had given me the opportunity to open stores in Puerto Rico. I was tired of running my own stores, and being a part of PMI would give me the ability to expand my holdings by owning stock in the company. I was the only franchise owner who had the right to go public, something I had negotiated with the Carney brothers from the outset. Pizza Hut was a young company at the time, and the Carney brothers were willing to give me that right in exchange for my ability to help them grow their business. Over the years, I remained the only franchise owner with the right to go public. Having the right to go public was a godsend for the company. We could buy out other franchisees and acquire new territories, allowing us to expand dramatically by using stock instead of money. I became the executive vice president of PMI, a position I held until PepsiCo bought Pizza Hut many years later.

The Out of Bounds restaurant in Fort Collins continued to do well, and the original owners, Ed Massey and Bill James, knew it. They had opened a new restaurant in Boulder, Colorado, named Around the Corner. That restaurant was successful, and they had expanded to three or four stores in Colorado. Bill and Ed approached me to help them develop the country, and I signed an agreement for a five-state territory: Texas, Arizona, Oklahoma, Kansas, and New Mexico, a territory they gave me at no cost. I would own the stores and pay them the 2 to 3 percent franchise fees on gross sales. I had everything to gain and nothing to lose, so I agreed to be their first franchisee.

I went to Phoenix, Arizona, and bought a home, as I knew I would be spending a lot of time there getting my franchises going. Within a year or so, I had built five stores around Scottsdale and Phoenix, all of which were profitable. Bill and Ed couldn't believe it! I had more stores open at that point than they did. It looked as if this would be a successful venture, but one thing I noticed whenever I was with Bill and Ed began to bother me. They used to come down to Phoenix, and we'd go out partying. I liked both of these good-looking, smart young men, but I noticed that they never mentioned business in their conversations. Over the years, I had made many friends who were franchise owners, and whenever we were together socially, eventually, we would talk about business. The fact that they never mentioned business was a red flag for me. I could see they weren't running a business but were just partying and raising hell, and I didn't want to be part of a losing deal. I wasn't just concerned; I was afraid that this company was not in good hands.

I decided to sell Bill and Ed back the rights to my restaurants. They had to assume all the debt, and they paid me about $350,000 for the rights. I hadn't paid them any franchise fees up front, so I got out of that deal money ahead. Sadly, Bill and Ed's company went bankrupt within two years of my leaving. Ironically, Bill and Ed had been offered millions for their franchise rights a year or so earlier by a Chinese firm, and they had turned the offer down, believing that their company was going to eventually be worth $100 million.

Sometimes you have to trust your intuition. I could read the handwriting on the wall; these guys were not in business to be in business. It is fine to have fun; I used to have more fun than is allowed by law, but I never forgot where I came from and how hard I had to work to get there. My business brain is turned on 24–7 no matter what I am doing, and when my brain tells me to run for the hills, I go. Bill and Ed should have taken the offer of millions for their franchise rights, set themselves up financially, and looked for the next deal. Knowing when to hold 'em and when to fold 'em is a sound business practice that will serve you well.

Chapter 13

During the year I was in Phoenix, my Realtor suggested I meet her hairdresser, a beautiful and sweet young woman whom she thought I might like. The Realtor didn't know if her hairdresser would be interested in going on a blind date, but the young woman agreed to go out with me if the three of us went together. A few nights later, my hairdresser introduced me to Robinette Suzanne Garvin. Robin was a very attractive woman with gorgeous red hair and green eyes. We had dinner at a French restaurant and enjoyed getting to know one another. I was immediately impressed with her sweet and unassuming nature. She was a classy young lady, and I was definitely interested in seeing her again. The next morning, my Realtor called and said, "You won't have any trouble getting a date with Robin!" I couldn't wait to see her, so I called Robin for a date with just the two of us that night.

For the next several weeks, we dated, and I knew I had found the woman of my dreams. I was struck by her; I was a goner, as the saying goes. One night, I invited friends over to my house to meet Robin. Robin was dressed in a beautiful white linen suit, but when she returned from a trip to the bathroom, she was soaking wet from head to foot. Apparently, when she went to the toilet, she looked over, saw a bidet, and, not knowing what it was, turned on the faucet. The water shot to the ceiling and rained down on her head. She was mortified and had to clean up and put on some dry clothes. I found the incident endearing. She was so cute and innocent!

Within a month, Robin moved into my home in Paradise Valley, and we made plans for her to come to my home in Fort Collins so that I could show her my life in Colorado. Several weeks later, she arrived in Colorado, and I took her to see the Out of Bounds restaurant. When we talked about her moving to Colorado to be with me, she got teary and said, "But, Wally, I'll be up here working in your restaurant, and you'll be traveling all over on business, and I'll never see you."

"Honey," I said, "that's not what I have in mind." I knew at that point I wanted to marry Robin, but I was concerned. Robin was only twenty-six years old, and I was forty-seven. With a twenty-one-year age difference, I was not sure she'd have me. We went back to Phoenix together, and shortly after, I got the courage to ask Robin to marry me. When she said yes, we immediately began planning our wedding.

Lorrie and I had been separated for seven years, but now that I was going to get married, I needed to get a divorce. I thought this would be an easy task, as Lorrie and I had never even talked about reconciling. We had lived entirely separate lives all those years. Our separation agreement had set Lorrie up financially for life, and I always had honored our agreement. Unfortunately, I was wrong. When Lorrie found out I was going to remarry, she sued me for half of my earnings during our seven-year separation on top of what I had already given her. I wanted to get the legal battle over with, so I offered her some Pizza Hut stock, which she and her lawyer refused to take. Eventually, we went to court, and when the judge saw all that Lorrie had gotten in our original settlement, he ruled in my favor. She should have taken the stock. Years later, it was worth over $2 million.

When I married Lorrie, we went to the justice of the peace in Cheyenne, Wyoming, and fifteen minutes later, we walked out married. This time, it would be different. Robin and I planned to get married at my home in Paradise Valley, and we invited about a hundred of our friends and relatives. My children, now grown, all came in from Colorado to be at the wedding. We had our home decorated to the hilt with flowers and hired the band from our favorite restaurant to play. Robin looked stunning on our wedding day, and I could not have been happier if I'd tried. It was the best day of my life.

Robin let me plan the honeymoon, and I was pleased to be able to treat my new bride to a trip we would both never forget. Shortly after the wedding, we got on a plane and headed to New York City, the first leg of our month-long trip. I had a limousine pick us up at the airport and take us to the Plaza Hotel. The Plaza Hotel is a world-famous luxury hotel and historic landmark on Central Park in Manhattan. Kings, presidents, movie stars, sports heroes, and business executives from all over the world have stayed at the Plaza since it opened near the turn of the century. Now Robin and I had a suite there. The hotel was so luxurious; it was the perfect place to spend a romantic week in New York. I hired a driver to show us the city, and we ate at some of New York's finest restaurants. When we took a horse-drawn carriage through Central Park, it was like a scene out of a romantic movie. We were crazy in love, and I am sure anyone who saw us knew it.

Our next stop was London, and in this case, getting there was half the fun. I had booked us on the Concorde, a supersonic airliner that would get us to London in half the time, an extraordinary flying experience I wanted to share with Robin. The Concorde was well appointed, and the service was first class all the way. When we sat down, a stewardess came by, put slippers on our feet, and put cookies on our trays but told us we couldn't eat them until she told us it was okay. After the plane took off and they turned on the turbo jets, she told us we could have our cookies. That turned out to be a joke on us, as we were accelerating so quickly that we could not lift our arms from our sides to get the cookies. The Concorde travels at Mach 2—over 1,300 miles an hour, breaking the sound barrier. Our travel time to London was just three and a half hours.

During the flight, Robin got "that look" in her eye and suggested I meet her in the bathroom. It was my honeymoon, we had had some champagne, and I thought her suggestion sounded like a great idea. We had our rendezvous, joining not the mile-high club but the ten-mile high club, as the Concorde flew at fifty-six thousand feet—a club, I suspect, with very few members. When I opened the door to go back to my seat, a woman was standing outside the door and looked at me knowingly with a smile on her face. I was embarrassed, as I was sure she knew what we were up to.

In London, we stayed at the Grosvenor House in the heart of Central London, just a block from Buckingham Palace. The Grosvenor House looked like a palace itself, and fresh fruit, flowers, and champagne awaited us in our suite. We may not have been royal, but they certainly made us feel that way! Our driver showed us the highlights of London, and we visited the Tower, the London Bridge, and Westminster Abbey and saw the changing of the guard at the palace. The driver pointed out a men's club where no women were allowed. That was enough for me! I told the driver to pull over, as I was taking Robin into the men's club. The driver said, "You can't do that."

"Really?" I said. "Watch me." I grabbed Robin's hand, and in we walked. I told the bartender that my wife and I were on our honeymoon from the United States, and I wanted Robin to see a men's club in London.

"Sure, no problem," he said.

I love a challenge and couldn't let no be the answer. I have found that usually all you have to do is ask, and most of the time, people are willing to bend the rules. We enjoyed our stay in London, and we looked forward to our next stop: Monaco.

Monaco is a tiny principality on the coast of the French Riviera, one of the world's smallest countries. Monte Carlo has long been a tourist destination for the rich and famous, with the mild climate, beautiful scenery, and casinos drawing wealthy visitors from around the world. I had visited Monte Carlo many years earlier with my friend Bill Fildes, and I knew Robin would love everything Monte Carlo had to offer. We stayed at Loew's Monte Carlo, a fairly modern hotel with rooms overlooking the Mediterranean Sea—the same hotel I had stayed in during my previous visit. I had gambled and spent a good deal of money with them and had thoroughly enjoyed my stay there. I knew Robin would be impressed. I wired a good amount of money to the cage of Loew's casino before we arrived, ensuring good service. The week flew by as we enjoyed sightseeing, lounging in the sunshine, shopping, and eating at fine restaurants. One evening, I wandered down to the casino while Robin was getting ready for dinner. Thirty minutes later, I returned to the room and surprised Robin with a pile of cash on the table. I won $7,000 in just half an hour! When we checked out at the end of the week, the woman at the desk said, "That will be seven dollars and fifty cents."

I told her, "That can't be right. We've been here a week in one of your suites and have eaten in your restaurants several times."

"No, that is correct," she said. "We have comped your honeymoon here, but we are not allowed to pay for your phone calls." Seven dollars and fifty cents for a week in Monte Carlo? That was a bargain, to say the least! I thought paying for our stay was a classy thing for the hotel to do and a good way to build customer loyalty.

We spent our last week in Lucerne, Switzerland, a city situated on Lake Lucerne. We had a beautiful room in a fine hotel, but when we walked in the door and saw that the room had twin beds, we immediately summoned the maids, who pushed our beds together and made it a king bed. It was our honeymoon after all! We enjoyed walking the city and crossing the Chapel Bridge, the oldest bridge in Europe, built in the fourteenth century. We rented a yacht and toured Lake Lucerne, impressed with the many beautiful castles overlooking the lake. The scenery was breathtaking—the lake surrounded by the Alps, wildflowers on the hills, and Alpine villages scattered throughout the area. We ate fish at a quaint fisherman's village, a perfect way to end the day on the lake. With reluctance, we ended our stay in Lucerne and boarded a plane back to the States. Our honeymoon over, it was now time for our real life together to begin.

My honeymoon with Robin is a trip I will never forget. I was proud to be able to provide Robin with the best of everything. I had come a long way from the days of hunting rabbits to put dinner on the table. This was a treat. Lifestyles of the rich and famous—me? The kid from Sweet Springs, Missouri? I couldn't believe my good fortune or that I even had one. I do know this. I had worked hard for twenty-five years to get to this point, and being able to treat the one I loved to this dream vacation was worth every minute of what it had taken to get there.

Chapter 14

After Robin and I returned from our honeymoon, we settled into my townhome in Fort Collins and began the next chapter of our lives. I immediately returned to work, and Robin began adjusting to her new life in Colorado. After I merged my Pizza Hut stores with Pizza Hut Management Inc., I did not need to travel to open new stores or oversee the operations of the Pizza Huts I owned, as the corporation located in San Antonio, Texas, now did that. With six thousand employees, management could address any problems, and I was free to concentrate on my other businesses.

I was, however, a hands-on owner of the Out of Bounds restaurant in Fort Collins and went in four or five days a week during lunch or dinner to greet customers, check on inventories, and make sure the food and service we provided were excellent. The restaurant continued to be very popular, and I knew that loyal customers were my best advertisers. I often picked up tabs for customers, knowing they would appreciate the gesture of me buying their meal, which would be more effective than spending the same money for advertising. Not only that, but I loved doing it! I always enjoyed getting to know my customers, and I became personal friends with many of them. People love to be recognized. I like to be treated well when I go out, and I tried to do the same for my customers.

I continued to oversee the operations of my cattle ranch in Wyoming and the breeding and sale of the Chianina cattle we had imported from Italy many years before. I also continued to buy and sell commercial real estate. I enjoyed the work and the challenge of putting deals together. Putting together a good deal is like putting together a puzzle. Once I put all the pieces in place, I could make my vision a reality. I love figuring these things out; it's fun! I bought the northeast corner of Prospect and Lemay, had it rezoned, started a development that later included a medical center, and sold it for a tidy sum. I bought a corner downtown and did the same. I never bit off more than I could chew. I favored smaller deals in the several-hundred-thousand-dollar range rather than getting into million-dollar deals and risking financial trouble if the deals went bad. Going bankrupt in the early days taught me a lot, and I patiently looked for any deal I thought would be profitable rather than a risky deal that might either make a large profit or fail entirely.

I handled my investment portfolio with the same mind-set. Unless you are an expert in the stock market, you should always hire a good broker. Even though I was somewhat of an expert after all of my years in the investment business, I still hired a broker to help me. I did some of my own trading but was frequently involved with my broker. People can't know market movements unless they make it their full-time job, and I wanted to be free to manage my other businesses. Being aware of your own limitations in both expertise and time is important, and maintaining a healthy investment portfolio required collaboration with a broker whose full-time job was knowing the market and making suggestions for which stocks I should buy and which ones I should sell. That partnership has served me well over the years.

After several years in the town house, Robin and I eventually found a house we wanted to buy in Fort Collins on Warren Lake. When we settled on the price, I wrote a check for the house. I only bought houses I could afford and always paid for them up front. I wanted the security of knowing my home and cars were paid for. I will never understand people who live above their means and are mortgaged to the hilt no matter how much money is coming in. I guess coming from where I came from made me determined to always ensure the financial stability of my family and shield them from harm should hard times come along.

The Warren Lake home was a beautiful bi-level home, and when we moved in, we remodeled and decorated to make it our own. We quickly discovered one of the downsides to being on the lake: we had a small backyard, and trash and papers would blow in from the lake whenever a north wind blew. I wanted to make my backyard larger, add a patio, and put some railroad ties in to keep the trash out of the yard. I went to the city to get a permit to make my backyard larger, but they told me I could not add dirt to the lake and would have to keep my yard as it was. *Wait a minute*, I thought. *That might be the secret: they said I couldn't put dirt into the lake, but they didn't say I couldn't take dirt out of the lake.* I went home and hired a backhoe to excavate dirt from the lake to my backyard. I designed a great backyard, including a small island, and installed the railroad ties I needed. The city never said a word, and my handiwork remains to this day.

When fall came, we enjoyed looking at the autumn leaves and their beautiful colors reflected on the lake. As the air turned cooler, we had the furnace serviced and prepared to settle in for the winter. One night, both Robin and I went to bed early. My son Larry called, but we were both asleep and didn't answer. A short time later, he called back and still got no answer. Larry would usually have assumed we were out for the evening and tried to reach us some other time, but on this occasion, he tried a third time. That call saved our lives.

Robin heard the phone ring the third time and got out of bed to answer the phone. She could barely walk. She was dizzy and disoriented. When she answered the phone, Larry knew immediately that something was wrong. He told her to dial 911 and open the front door. Robin did as instructed, and before long, paramedics arrived on the scene. I was unconscious and unaware that I was within minutes of dying. My fingernails were black, and I was unresponsive. Robin and I were both taken by ambulance to the hospital, where the diagnosis of carbon monoxide poisoning was made. Our situation was so dire that we were immediately airlifted to a hospital in Denver that had a hyperbaric chamber to put us in. A hyperbaric chamber has three times as much oxygen as normal air, and it was the treatment we desperately needed. Robin and I were both critically ill and spent ten days in the hospital and many months at home recovering. We found out later that when we had our furnace serviced, the technician set the internal thermostat too high. It was a close call, and we were both lucky to have survived. The company eventually compensated us for their mistake, but nothing we got could make up for our struggle back from the brink of death.

After my recovery, I met a man in the oil business who had leased oil property north of Greeley, Colorado, with a couple of other oilmen, and he wanted me to get into the deal. They were in the process of digging their first well, and I agreed to buy a sixteenth interest for a couple thousand dollars. It didn't take me long to see that things were not being done properly, and I knew I would have to be in control of how things were being done or get out entirely. I decided to buy out the original investors and start running the business myself. I formed Noel Exploration and began finding investors for the oil field.

Investors buy shares of the lease and shoulder the expense of drilling the wells. If the wells hit, oil can be a lucrative investment, but it's a gamble. The potential for cash flow lasting a decade or more and the tax incentives attract many investors who are willing to take the risk. The rancher who owned the land got a sixteenth interest for free, and my company received another sixteenth for operating the field and putting the deal together.

It takes several weeks to get the leases and hire a drilling company with the heavy equipment and knowledge of the drilling process. I hired a reputable drilling company out of Denver to drill the well, set up the tanks, and get the well ready for production. Once the well has been determined to be a producer, they bring in the storage tanks and complete the well. Over the next two years, we drilled sixteen wells and struck oil in every well! I hired my father-in-law to manage the company and oversee daily operations. After several years of my oil field pumping so-called black gold, an oil company from back east approached me, and I sold them the oil field for a healthy profit.

Although I ran a variety of businesses, the same business principles apply to all: show up, work hard, pay your bills, solve minor problems before they become major problems, have integrity in every transaction, treat investors honestly, maintain good credit, be respectful, and know that what goes around comes around. Adhering to those principles absolutely will lead you on the road to success.

Chapter 15

With a beautiful wife by my side and my business life going well, I felt on top of the world. I was always busy; driven by the engine of the past, I never wasted a moment trying to get ahead and stay ahead. In my late forties, I was a man in his prime—still young enough to work hard and play hard, I wanted to do it all. I was usually up before five, going nonstop through the day and sometimes well into the night. I didn't have any inclination to slow down. Slow down? I had never even considered the idea. Occasionally, I would get more breathless than I thought I should, but I didn't give it much thought. I figured I was just a little out of shape—too much good food, an extra glass of wine, or the couple of extra pounds I was carrying. I could still do all my normal activities, and I wasn't worried.

Robin, however, became concerned when she noticed my breathlessness whenever I exerted myself, and I finally agreed to get checked out. We made an appointment with my doctor, and after he listened to my symptoms and checked me over, he sent me for a treadmill test. When I failed the treadmill test, he sent me to the hospital for some additional testing. The tests determined that my left coronary artery was totally obstructed. I was scheduled for a balloon angioplasty, and the doctor told us I would be out in a short time. However, after repeated attempts, they could not get the heart catheter past a certain point, and the doctor came out and told Robin that they had staff waiting and that I needed open-heart surgery immediately.

Robin began crying hysterically, unprepared for this sudden turn of events. I saw her only briefly as they wheeled me down the hall toward the surgery center. The doctor asked me, "Would you like a priest to give you your last rites?"

"No, thanks," I answered. "If I haven't done it right by now, between here and the door isn't going to change anything."

The surgeons opened my chest and my leg where they took a vein to graft around the blocked artery. It turned out that my artery was totally occluded and, like a crimped garden hose, not letting the blood through. My heart was not getting the blood it needed, and I was lucky to have not dropped dead of a heart attack.

After spending ten days in the hospital, I was released with some advice from the doctor: "You need to slow down, Wally!" Within a few weeks, I felt great! I was climbing ladders and doing much more than the doctor had advised during my recovery. Once I was past the initial healing, I felt better than I had in years. I had not realized how much better I'd feel once my heart was getting the blood it needed. *Slow down, Wally!* The idea certainly didn't come naturally.

Robin and I talked, and we decided that I did need to slow down, but we would need to be in a quiet place for me to be able to do it. We decided to move out to a ranch eighteen miles north of town we had bought while living in the town house. We used to go to our Bonner Peak Ranch to ride horses, have picnics, and enjoy the outdoors. The ranch had a house that we had used for a getaway but could easily have been used as our full-time residence. Within a month of my surgery, we packed up our house and moved to the Bonner Peak Ranch.

Over the next several months, I began to let go of the frenetic pace I had kept up over the years. I started selling some of my businesses and stopped dealing in commercial real estate. I continued to run the Out of Bounds, but with a great manager, I did not have to go in if I didn't want to. We were not so far out of town that we couldn't go into Fort Collins for dinner and to socialize, so we weren't entirely cut off from the outside world.

Even though Robin was a city girl, she loved life at the ranch. She was never entirely comfortable on the horses after one bucked her off, but she rode with me often. I loved saddling up one of my horses and riding around the eighty-acre ranch and into Roosevelt National Forest, which the ranch adjoined. My favorite horse, Joey, was so much fun to ride. He had a lot of spirit, but he didn't misuse it. Once I got over the saddle of the first range, there was a valley with acres and acres carpeted with brilliant wildflowers. I would ride down into the valley of color, get off Joey, remove his saddle and bridle, and turn him loose. Robin usually fixed me a lunch, and I would sit down on the ground, have my lunch, and watch Joey graze around me. It was quiet, I was quiet, and I finally allowed myself to heal.

Over the next year, we fixed up the house and added a three-car garage for our cars. We built a barn and a round pen to break horses and were then able to bring our thirty quarter horses, which we had boarded elsewhere, to the ranch. I had a pond dug on the property so that our horses always had a supply of water. We hired a trainer who looked after the horses and trained them for races. We entered our horses in many horse races, from the Denver Stock Show to numerous state and county fairs in the western states' racing circuits. We loved traveling to watch our horses race and make informal bets with the other owners. Horse racing is more than a hobby; it is a passion born of the love of horses, the love of competition, and the love of winning.

The City of Fort Collins approached me to sell them the County Square, a quarter of a city block I had bought years earlier, which included the building in which the Out of Bounds was located. The city was buying up property to eventually expand their municipal office space. I told them I would consider selling but wanted a long-term lease for the Out of Bounds to protect the jobs of the employees who worked there and to continue to get paid on my investment. We negotiated a price, which I made sure included the extraordinary expenses I had incurred meeting the city code restrictions when I built the outdoor patio at the restaurant years earlier. I also required that a future buyer could assume the lease. The city met my demands, much to my delight, and we closed the deal.

Several months later, I sold the Out of Bounds to a restaurateur who had managed some of MGM's restaurants. During the next year, he let the business fail, skipped town, and filed for bankruptcy. He had taken a successful and highly profitable business and run it into the ground in less than a year, proving that what looks easy is not easy. In the restaurant business, you are only as successful as your last meal served. If the quality of the food and service goes downhill and the prices go up, your business will vanish overnight. It did.

Robin and I were in town dining at another restaurant, when an acquaintance let me know that the city was going to try to make me pay this guy's rent! "Those chickenshits," I said, "know I don't owe them the money; that restaurant was sold!" I was hot, so I hired a crew, went to the restaurant, and took all the furnishings and fixtures out of the building and stored them. I then called the city and let them know they could have their building back.

When the owner skipped town, he had not paid the employees' withholding taxes. Most of those employees had worked for me, so I went ahead and paid them. I also had previously taken out a bank loan for $200,000 for renovations to the restaurant, which the new owner had assumed. When he filed bankruptcy, the loan would have to be written off, but I felt bad that the bank would end up having to eat a loan I had taken. I always pay my debts, and even though this debt was no longer mine, I went ahead and paid it anyway.

In the business world, keeping your good name is vital if you want to continue doing business. There are few people out there who would not be willing to do business with me again. Over the years, whomever I dealt with learned to trust my word and know that I am not underhanded and do not try to cheat people. If you do burn your bridges, don't plan on being in business long. Your bad reputation will haunt you, and that will get you nowhere fast.

Chapter 16

On the surface, everything seemed to be going well. Robin and I were doing what we had set out to do. My health crisis had passed, and I was no longer caught up in running so many businesses and putting together real-estate deals, but I was beginning to get concerned about Robin. When I returned to the ranch after being in town, I would sometimes find her a little wobbly and slurring her words. I didn't see any evidence that anything was amiss, and most of the time, she seemed fine. When I asked her about it, she just said she felt a little off or was tired, and I let it go.

When her parents came to visit and Robin was out of the house, I told them of my concern. They immediately began searching the house, and what they found broke my heart. They produced bottles of alcohol hidden everywhere: under the mattress, in our closets, in the laundry room, and in drawers and cabinets. I don't know why their first instinct was to search the house. Perhaps Robin had had a problem years earlier—I didn't know, and I didn't ask. All I knew was that my wife had a serious problem, and now so did I. I had lost both my parents to alcohol, and I was determined that I would not lose my wife to addiction.

We confronted Robin when she returned home. While she admitted that she had a problem, she did not think she needed any help. I immediately locked up all the alcohol in the house and stopped drinking around Robin. That didn't stop her. She continued to find a way to have a stash of alcohol hidden somewhere. I insisted she go to counseling and Alcoholics Anonymous, and I attended meetings with her. After three or four tough months, Robin was able to get sober, and for the rest of our marriage, she never touched another drop off alcohol. Knowing that alcoholism destroys the lives of many people, I admired her strength and fortitude. I am not sure what I would have done if Robin had continued down that road, for I knew I was utterly powerless to stop her unless she wanted to get well. The demons of my past haunted me during those months with scenes from my childhood; I watched my mother and father in scene after drunken scene replaying in my head. I was more than relieved when my sweet, funny, wonderful wife reappeared once and for all.

Robin and I lived happily at the ranch for quite some time, but we both began to explore other possibilities. Even though I had completely recovered from my heart bypass surgery, Robin continued to worry about my health. Given our twenty-year age difference, I understood Robin's insistence that we enjoy every day we had together. I began to toy with the idea of retiring completely.

PepsiCo had bought out Pizza Hut several years earlier and had approached me several times to buy my stock in PMI and the remaining Pizza Hut stores I owned outright. Because I had negotiated the right to go public into my contract years earlier, PepsiCo had to negotiate with me separately. All the other franchise owners had gotten whatever PepsiCo had offered in the initial sales agreement, as Pizza Hut had the first right of refusal of their stores, and they couldn't sell to anyone else. At this point, I was ready to sell my Pizza Hut stock, but I didn't want cash. I wanted to be bought out on regulation 144a, rolling my several hundred thousand shares of PMI stock into Pepsi stock. The Pepsi stock would continue to appreciate until I was ready to sell. Additionally, if I held the stock for two years, I would not pay ordinary income tax on the earnings but, rather, capital gains, giving me a significant tax advantage. I negotiated the sales of my individual stores separately and got twenty times earnings for each store. What had begun twenty years earlier with a $5,000 investment became a multimillion dollar sale and secured my financial future for the rest of my life.

I completed the deal with PepsiCo over the phone while at the ranch. When I hung up the phone, I was elated. Everything I had worked for all those years was now a reality. I was done; I had done it! I flashed back to my years in the coast guard, watching with awe the wealthy people on Mackinaw Island and wanting to be like them. I hadn't just seen their lifestyle and wished I could have it but, rather, had wanted to have it in a way that motivated me to pursue it. Of course, at the time, I'd had no way of knowing how I was going to get there; I had just been determined that someday I would—and now I had. I'll admit it—I was driven, but that drive and willingness to do whatever I needed to do to be successful had paid off. I found Robin, and we celebrated the closing of the biggest deal of my life.

Robin and I began to contemplate what our future might look like now that I was going to retire. We could do anything we wanted to do and live anywhere we wanted to live. Over the years, Robin and I had traveled to

Texas many times when I went to the PMI headquarters in San Antonio on business. We began to talk about buying a place in Texas near water so that I could finally buy the yacht I had always wanted. We made several trips to Texas to begin looking at different towns that might offer what we were looking for. First, I had many business deals going that I needed to wrap up in Colorado, and years would go by before we would make our move.

Several years passed, and my bank in Fort Collins, which had both my personal and business accounts, apparently got into some financial trouble and began calling in some of their larger loans. I had a half-million-dollar loan with them for some commercial property I owned, and when they called me to come down to the bank for a meeting, I anticipated what was going to happen. I knew I would have to sell my Pepsi stock to come up with the money to pay off the loan, but because two years had passed since I had taken Pepsi's offer, I was now able to sell their stock and cash out. The financial officer took me into his office and, with a smug look on his face, told me they were calling in the loan or would have to foreclose. He said, "So what are you going to do, Wally?"

"Well," I replied, "I'm going to get out my checkbook and write you a check for the remaining balance on my loan."

He got silent and just stared at me, not knowing, of course, of the thousands of shares of Pepsi stock I had just sold. I got out my checkbook, wrote the bank a check, and handed it to him. After he looked at it with his mouth open, I explained why I was able to come up with that amount so quickly. When he saw the check from Pepsi and the amount of money that would remain after paying off the loan, he asked, "What account do you want us to put the rest of the money in, Wally?"

"I'm going to walk out the door and deposit the money in an account at the bank across the street!" I replied curtly. After years of doing business with this bank, I didn't appreciate the banker's attitude when he thought they had me in a tight spot and would soon be owning my property. *Fine*, I thought, *I'll just take my business elsewhere*, and that was exactly what I did.

I don't understand businessmen who blow up long-term relationships for short-term gains. When you have good customers, it pays to keep them, no matter what business you are in. If you are in business for the long haul, maintaining relationships over time is key. You never know when you might need some of those contacts. What goes around comes around, and word of mouth travels. Alienated customers can harm your business and diminish your ability to stay profitable when times are tough.

Chapter 17

After several more visits to Texas, Robin and I decided to buy a home in Kemah, Texas, a small community on Kemah Lake with access to Galveston Bay. The community has fewer than two thousand full-time residents but is home to one of the largest pleasure boat fleets in the United States. It is a charming town with beautiful waterfront properties, great restaurants, and plenty of retail shops. Kemah draws tourists from all over the Houston and Galveston areas and is anything but sleepy. The town had everything we needed, and we found a beautiful three-story home to buy on the water in the yacht club.

We made our final arrangements, put the ranch on the market, and left Fort Collins for a new life on the Gulf Coast. Robin and I wanted to live an exciting life with ability to go and do when we felt like it. We never felt tied to a home or a piece of property. Because we had each other, home was wherever we wanted it to be, and that gave us great freedom to live in any number of locations. We thought we'd try life on the Gulf, but if we didn't like it, we would simply move somewhere else.

After we got settled, we enjoyed shopping for furniture and decorating our new home. The house had large windows overlooking the lake, and an observation tower with a telescope at the top of the house. We had fun watching the boats and yachts come and go throughout the day. There was always something to see when we looked out the windows, and we were constantly entertained. The boats were so close we felt like we were living in the middle of the yacht club.

We searched for a yacht to buy and, after trying out many different boats, settled on a sixty-five-foot Carver twin-engine yacht. This luxury yacht had two staterooms, a walk-in shower, a full navigation system, and all the amenities we could possibly want. Robin wanted to name the yacht the *Out of Bounds*, so we did. We had a blast cruising the lake and going into Galveston Bay. We'd dock and eat at fine restaurants on the water and could either spend the night on the yacht or make an easy trip back to our house. We met many wonderful friends who would accompany us on our boat, or we would go on theirs for lunch, dinner, or cocktails. It was a lifestyle that was easy to love. We docked our yacht at the Kemah Lake Yacht Club until I had a dock built at our home, and then we had easy access to come and go whenever we pleased.

Robin and I lived the good life as a retired couple for many months. We filled our days golfing at the country club, fishing on Kemah Lake and Galveston Bay, socializing with our friends, cruising the waterways in our yacht, and traveling when we needed a change of pace. We continued to spend time in Scottsdale, Arizona, staying at our townhome that we bought shortly after we married. We always enjoyed our time in Arizona, visiting with both family and friends. Scottsdale was our home away from home, and we often flew to Arizona when we needed a change of pace.

Roy Herberger and his wife, Pam, were friends of ours in Arizona, and we often got together with them when Robin and I came to town. Dr. Herberger was a bright and capable businessman who, at the time, was the president of Thunderbird University, a graduate school of international management. We enjoyed conversing about business whenever we met. We had a lot in common, having both been involved in a variety of businesses during our careers. Our educational backgrounds, however, could not have been more different. While Dr. Herberger held a PhD in business and marketing, I was a high-school dropout with little formal education; however, forty years of business experience provided me with all the business education I needed, and our business experiences provided us with a wide variety of topics to discuss. He respected my opinions and was impressed with all I had accomplished in my career.

During one of our conversations, Dr. Herberger mentioned Massimo da Milano, a company in which he was both a stockholder and an outside director on the Massimo board. Massimo da Milano was a small chain of Italian restaurants in the Dallas area that included a bakery supplying the individual stores and almost three hundred commercial accounts. He told me that Massimo had filed for Chapter 11 bankruptcy protection, citing liabilities of $2.3 million and assets of $1.1 million in the court filing. Roy said the situation had continued to deteriorate when the state of Texas had sought $70,000 in unpaid sales taxes and had asked the bankruptcy court to convert Massimo's case into a Chapter 7 bankruptcy. If that were to occur, the company's assets would be sold off and the proceeds distributed to creditors. Stockholders were on the brink of losing whatever money they had invested in this company, and that included my friend. Roy asked my opinion and wondered if there might be anything I could do to help. After we discussed the situation for some time, he asked if I could go down to Dallas to see if I could get the company out of bankruptcy.

At sixty-two, I was happily retired and reluctant to get involved, but I wanted to help my friend, and the situation presented me with an interesting challenge. Could I figure out a way to save this company? Trying to bring a company out of bankruptcy would be a huge time commitment if I took it on, and I mulled the situation over for several days before I agreed to go to Dallas to see what I could do.

Roy wrote me a letter of introduction so that the board of directors would allow me to examine their books, talk with the shareholders, and meet with the bankruptcy judge if I thought there was any possibility of turning this company around. Once I examined the books and visited a few stores, I could easily see why this company was losing money. The books made no sense; the company's profits were evaporating into thin air, which told me there was plenty of corruption going on. The stores were mismanaged, and those in charge were not addressing obvious problems. Having been in the restaurant business for a long time, I was able to evaluate the situation quickly. I believed it was possible to save this sinking ship, and I wanted to try.

With the blessing of the board, I made an appointment for a court hearing with the bankruptcy judge on this case. Judge Harold Abramson was a gruff, no-nonsense kind of judge who, I surmised, thought this hearing was a waste of his time. He asked me to take the stand and began questioning me. "You know you can't take a salary," he said.

I told the judge I didn't want a salary but would take stock in the company. I wanted one-third ownership of Massimo Inc. if I got them out of bankruptcy. "If I don't," I said, "nobody owes me a dime."

"You know they're dead ducks," he said, "so if you do manage to get this company out of bankruptcy, I think what you are asking is reasonable."

After the court hearing, I knew I had my work cut out for me and would be spending a great deal of time in Dallas, getting this company turned around. I spoke with Robin, and we immediately searched for a furnished apartment for us to use when I needed to be in Dallas.

I now had complete control of the company, and I knew the first order of business was to stop the hemorrhaging and begin paying the long-overdue bills. I slashed the overhead by reducing the corporate headquarter payroll by 80 percent and cut the number of restaurant workers by twenty-five people. I replaced senior management by firing three of the five restaurant managers and then offered the two remaining managers and three new managers 15 percent interest in their stores, just as I had with Pizza Hut. My biggest challenge, however, was persuading all the vendors to extend Massimo credit once again so that the company could remain in business. All the vendors had Massimo on a cash-only basis because the company was in bankruptcy and previous bills were still unpaid. The vendors knew Massimo was going under, and extending credit at that point would be like throwing money out the window. I had to convince them otherwise.

I called all the vendors in for a meeting with me. There were both small local vendors and large national vendors, including companies such as Kraft Foods. I explained what I had done so far and explained what I planned to do to turn the company around. I had to negotiate a deal with these vendors, or we could not stay in business. Paying cash for every delivery was impossible not only because that method was inefficient but also because cash transactions increased the risk of theft on both sides. The vendors around the conference table listened to what I had to say, and after I answered any questions they had, they agreed to extend the company credit.

With the vendors on board and the overhead slashed, I now needed to figure out how to make this company profitable. The profit and loss numbers shown on the books made no sense, and I had known it the minute I first looked at them several months before. I knew the bakery should be profitable, as Massimo delivered baked goods to hundreds of restaurants and hotels in the Dallas metro area. I knew the issue wasn't just bad management; there had to be people stealing from the company, and I was determined to get to the bottom of it.

My next move made perfect sense to me, but most business schools probably don't teach it. In the evenings, after normal operating hours, I would hide on the dock of the bakery and wait to see what might be going on after dark. Sure enough, I discovered that trucks were pulling up to the dock, and product was flying out the back door. Not only were employees giving product to friends and family, but also, it turned out there was a phony subsidiary company set up by one of the head bakers, who was selling product under his own company name using

Massimo products and baked goods. He even had labels printed saying he was a distributor of Massimo. I am sure this was a profitable venture for the head baker, but it was the primary reason the bakery was losing money and, of course, was highly illegal. I promptly fired the employees involved and pursued legal action against them. After I took care of that matter, the bakery became profitable. I had a hard time believing that no one in management had discovered this large-scale theft before I did, but they had not.

I found plenty of other examples of mismanagement. The fleet of trucks used to deliver the goods typically had fuel costs that were out of line and also had other cost overruns. The company was not holding the drivers accountable for any of the excess expenses. When I asked about it, the person in charge agreed that there was a problem but didn't know how to combat it. Because deliveries had to be made and when confronted, each driver blamed the other, he was at a loss. I said, "Well, number the trucks and assign that truck to one person. That driver is responsible for his truck: the expenses, deliveries, and products to be delivered. That will stop the funny business with the trucks." The supervisor followed up on my directive, and sure enough, the expenses immediately came in line. Accountability is essential in business, and this company had operated for years with few accountability systems in place. No wonder this company was going bankrupt!

I made changes at the restaurants, dropping some of the less-popular items on the menu and emphasizing the hot, freshly prepared pastas, salads, and baked goods. We also made changes to the service and decor and added full-service dining in the evenings. Customers began to return, and the decline in sales turned around.

Robin and I spent much of our time in Dallas during those months, but in four months, the company emerged from bankruptcy protection, and in less than a year, the company was once again profitable. That was big news in the industry, and articles in the *Dallas Morning News* and *Restaurant News*, the restaurant industry's largest publication, highlighted the turnaround that I had orchestrated. It was a feather in my cap, and I was proud of what I had done. However, I didn't want to stay in Dallas, running the company indefinitely. I had done what I'd set out to do, and it was time to go home. Robin and I returned to Kemah, looking forward to waking up each day and once again deciding what we wanted to do to entertain ourselves.

Unfortunately, once I left Massimo, the company returned to its former ways and eventually went under. That was a shame. I didn't bring anything to the company that anyone with some leadership skills, hard work, and common sense couldn't have replicated. I was willing to do what I needed to do, including my own detective work, to make this company successful. Do many company presidents go undercover to find out what's going on? Maybe not, but if your company is losing money, somebody needs to do it. I am not above doing any job that needs to be done. If you are going to lead the troops, you'd better be willing to spend some time in the trenches. Better that than losing the war.

Chapter 18

Once Robin and I returned to Kemah, Texas, we fell into the rhythm of our lives before Massimo. We enjoyed reconnecting with all of our friends and resuming our social lives. Robin and I golfed at the club several days a week and took the *Out of Bounds* out almost every day. We also wanted to travel, as we had only made trips between Dallas and home for seven months. For the next year and a half, we did just that. We enjoyed our home, our friends, our boat, our travel adventures, and each other. Robin and I were never apart, and we both liked it that way.

We took several fishing trips to Eagle Lake in Northwestern Ontario, Canada, to fish for walleye and northern pike. Eagle Lake is famous for its scenic beauty and its fantastic freshwater fishing. We stayed at either the North Shore or South Shore Lodge in private cabins scattered along the peninsula, which were rustic but beautiful. Robin had turned into quite the fisherman and was enthusiastic to get out on the lake every day to see what we might catch.

When we returned to Kemah, Robin began to complain that her neck was bothering her with pain that would not go away. We didn't know if the problem was too much golf or too much fishing but decided to get it checked out. Robin's doctor sent us to the MD Anderson Cancer Center in Houston to get some tests, and Robin was diagnosed with a herniated disc in her neck. She was given pain medication and was able to continue all the activities that she enjoyed.

We decided to go on a deep-sea fishing trip to Mazatlán, Mexico, where we hired a yacht and crew to take us sport fishing out in the Pacific. Mazatlán has some of the best sport fishing in the world, famed for its marlin-rich waters. We went out every day, and the fishing was awesome! We caught an amazing amount of fish. I landed a marlin, which is a huge thrill for any fisherman. Those fish are humungous and fight like hell! Robin caught a dolphin, which she struggled with for hours and damn near didn't get it in the boat. She was so tired that she wanted to quit, but I kept encouraging her to hang on, and she did! After the day of fishing, we ate seafood almost every night at a small oceanfront restaurant with fabulous food and a great band. Robin and

I always enjoyed our vacations together away from home, but we also loved returning to our beautiful home in Texas.

We were at the Kemah Country Club when we met Larry Bush and Charles Brown. Larry had a company that rented large industrial equipment, and Charles was an attorney. These two individuals became highly interested in me when they found out what I had done for a living before retiring. Larry and Charles were particularly fascinated with my involvement in Pizza Hut. They let me know that they were interested in getting into the franchise business, and I let them know I was not interested. Every time Robin and I saw them, they would pump me for information about the franchise industry. Once, after several conversations, Larry said to me, "Wally, I know you are not interested in getting into a franchise, but if you were going to get in one, which one would you choose?"

"Well," I said, "I've read a lot about and heard a lot about Papa John's Pizza. I think they've got a winner, but I think their areas are probably all sold out, at least any one you might want."

Every now and then, we'd see Larry and Charles, and they would continue the same line of questioning, now focused on Papa John's Pizza. They asked if I thought it was possible for them to get in. I answered honestly that without experience in the industry, I was highly doubtful that Papa John's would be interested, but they could try. "I don't think Papa John's wants mom-and-pop operations, but even if they do, you wouldn't want one. First, you would have to run the damn thing, and one Papa John's isn't going to be too exciting," I said.

"Well," they said, "what would you do if you were going to go do that?"

I said, "I'd want the East Coast or the West Coast—probably the West Coast would be the best—and I'd want at least a fifty-to-one-hundred-store development area to make it worthwhile. I'd also want two other things that they probably wouldn't do. I'd want the right to go public, and I'd want the first right of refusal for them to buy my territory taken out of the franchise agreement—and they're not going to do that."

The conversation continued on several more occasions, and privately, I said to Robin that it might be fun to get back into the business. You can only golf, fish, and boat so much, and we were still young. I wasn't bored exactly, but I have always found business to be

There Are No Bounds

both interesting and fun. I began to at least consider the idea of coming out of retirement. Larry and Charles kept after us, and finally, I said, "Let's have a meeting," so we did.

I invited Larry and Charles to my home so that we could talk about the possibility of working together on a franchise deal. Charles, the attorney, turned to me and said, "I checked around, and I don't think you started those companies, Wally. You might have been in them, but you didn't start them."

"What did you say?" I asked, annoyed. "Did I tell you I started them?"

"Well, yeah, you did," he replied.

"So you don't think I did that?" I asked.

"That's what I heard," he replied.

I got the files out and laid them right in front of him. I was the incorporator and president of those companies, and the documents in front of him proved it. He got a little pale, and I said, "There is no sense in us going any further if you think I'm not what I am supposed to be, so let's call this damn meeting off."

Larry got upset and told Charles and me to calm down and continue our meeting. They started getting serious, saying, "What would you want?" and "This is what we want." I figured that what I asked for would kill the deal. I wanted $200,000 per year, a house and a car paid for, 66 ⅔ of the stock, and no other officers in the company, and I would have the only vote. They said, "We'll do it!" If someone had said that to me, I'd have run like hell. I couldn't believe they agreed to it!

I said, "Well, you're the attorney—draw the agreement up!"

After I had signed the agreement, I said, "I'm warning you—we are going to go back to Louisville, and Papa John's is going to say no."

Robin and I flew to Louisville, Kentucky, to the Papa John's headquarters. I called and told them who I was, and they agreed to meet with me. Papa John's was a fairly new company at the time and was interested in growing their company. When Robin and I met with them, they asked what I would need to have if we were going to get together. "I want the greater Los Angeles area, between fifty and a hundred stores, the right to go public, and the first right of refusal you have in your franchise agreement taken out of ours."

John Schnatter, a great guy, was the president of the company. I was not as impressed with his brother, Chuck, a lawyer. After discussing our proposal and talking about the Papa John's organization, Chuck said, "Wally, we give our managers stock in our stores. What do you do?"

"So do I," I answered.

"How do you do yours?" he asked.

"I give my managers five percent a year for three years, giving them a maximum ownership of fifteen percent. If they leave the company, they have to sell me back the stock at book value, which, of course, will have increased."

"We let our managers keep the stock when they leave," he said.

"You do?" I said. "What if ten managers leave? You no longer own the store!"

"Oh" was all he managed to reply. I think he was embarrassed. This wasn't rocket science, and it should have been obvious to him, but sometimes lawyers do not make the best businessmen. I suspect that after I left, they changed their contracts with store managers to protect their company, but I don't know if they did. If not, it was their loss, not mine.

On the plane going home, I told Robin that we could forget this deal, as there was no way Papa John's was going to agree to my terms. I had asked for a great deal from them, and I knew it. However, I had been in this business for a long time, and if I was going to come out of retirement, it had to be worth my while. I also knew that I could make this company money if they agreed to my terms. The next day, they called to tell me they accepted my terms for the deal. We were back in business.

The great thing about not needing to make money was the ability to negotiate terms that were tilted in my favor. If my terms were not met, I could walk away and forget about it. I was always a good negotiator. I learned early in my career as an investment broker to read contracts, and when I do, I am always looking for things I would like rewritten to benefit my bottom line. Contracts are tedious, and many people don't bother reading the fine print, including the people at the table with whom you have come to negotiate. I have often come away with substantially more money in a deal because I asked for certain things to be written into or taken out of a contract before I would sign on the dotted line. Now I could ask for even more. I didn't need the money, but I did love the challenge of negotiating a deal.

Chapter 19

Once Papa John's, Larry Bush, Charles Brown, and I signed contracts, I formed a new company, PJ Management Inc., to operate this new venture. Incorporating provides many benefits, including personal asset protection, tax benefits, and deductible expenses. I was the president and CEO of the company but did not need an office or employees. The only help I needed would come from Robin, and she proved to have a natural instinct for business and was a great asset.

Robin and I flew to Los Angeles to look for a place to live. We kept our homes in Kemah and Scottsdale, as we intended to return to our retired lives once we had developed our territory. We also wanted to continue to stay at our home and spend time with our friends in Texas while we lived in California. After several days spent exploring the LA area, we settled on a beautiful furnished apartment on Orange Grove Boulevard in Pasadena, California, as our temporary home.

Once we took care of shutting down our home in Kemah and moving to Pasadena, we immediately began looking for locations for Papa John's restaurants. Within the first few weeks, we had several locations selected and began securing leases, renovating the stores, and hiring employees. The contractor we were working with suggested I hire Hector Ortiz if I could get him. He said Hector was a great guy who was competent and currently working in the franchise industry. I called Hector and asked him to come in for an interview. I immediately liked him and offered him a job. After we discussed the details of the job and its compensation package, Hector accepted my offer. Hector turned out to be one of the best managers I have ever hired.

When negotiating with potential landlords, I always asked for five-year leases with three options for renewal. That way, if the store was not successful, we wouldn't be stuck with a long-term lease. We also always got the right to assign the lease written into the contract. Many times, the landlord wanted rent plus a percentage of the profit, but we always said no. If they wanted us as tenants, rent was all they would get from us.

It takes about six months to go through the process of opening a store. Once we got the first store open, we used that store to train the crew for each successive store. Since it does not take long to get a pizza business started, it made sense to run double crews. That way, the minute the next store was ready, we'd have a trained crew ready to go and could open the new store. Robin was a great help, and she often had business ideas that amazed me.

GE Mortgage offered to lend me 110 percent of what I needed for each store if I would do all of my business with them, and I did. I didn't have to put up any of my own money to get the restaurants open. I just needed to make sure all my stores were profitable so that each one could easily make its loan payments. Finding great locations was the key. The stores needed to have high visibility and easy in-and-out access, with no one-way streets, if possible. Our partners, Larry and Charles and their wives, came to California for a few days, and as we showed them around Los Angeles, they pointed out what they thought were good locations. Robin and I were polite but laughed privately. They had no idea how to choose a good location, and their suggestions were awful. Choosing locations isn't just an art; it's a science. I always got all the demographic data I could get my hands on and poured over the data before I made a decision. I knew that one bad choice could hurt the company, and I always made sure I did my homework. By the end of our first year, Robin and I had ten to twelve stores open, all of which were profitable. Papa John's was proving to be a successful endeavor, and we were having a great time doing it.

Thunderbird University contacted me to speak at the 2000 Winterim Entrepreneurial CEO Seminar to their business graduate-school students. Each year, the conference highlights fifteen current and former industry leaders who are selected for their expertise and significant impact in their area of concentration. I felt honored to be among business's top board chairpersons, chief executive officers, and company presidents asked to speak. I spoke to the students about my background and eventual success in the business world. I did not need notes; this was my life. I spoke from my heart, and the students and faculty received my presentation well. I was a high-school dropout speaking to international business-school graduate students, which meant a great deal to me. I was humbled by the invitation and proud to be considered one of the top business leaders in the country. With our Papa John's franchises doing well and with a large territory for expansion, Robin and I decided to buy a home in California. We knew it would take many years to maximize the potential of the territory in this part of Southern California. We wanted to find a house that felt more like home to us, as we were now spending most of our time in California. The traffic and congestion in LA had started to wear on us, and we wanted a more tranquil environment. After looking at a number of possible locations and homes, we settled on a gorgeous one-level home on a golf course in Rancho Mirage, an upscale community of fewer than twenty thousand, located one hundred miles east of Los Angeles. In the heart of the Palm Springs Valley, it offered us everything we were looking for: a smaller community, fine restaurants, great views, and a peaceful setting.

Robin and I always enjoyed shopping for furniture and decorating our homes ourselves. We frequently received compliments about our places, and people often asked us who our decorator was. I don't know how I developed my sense of style; I certainly didn't grow up seeing tastefully decorated homes. However, over the years, I lived in many places and always had fun selecting furniture and accessories that fit the home and locale. Robin and I couldn't imagine letting someone else decorate for us, and our home in Rancho Mirage was no exception. Our place in Pasadena came fully furnished, so we were starting from scratch and got busy the minute we bought the house.

I commuted into Los Angeles several days a week to check on my existing stores and continue finding locations for new stores. Hector Ortiz was a great manager and did everything possible to keep things running smoothly. He knew the area well and often had done the legwork scouting new locations. Hector gave me great suggestions that often panned out, and we continued to open a new store every six to eight weeks.

I had come out of retirement and was thoroughly enjoying this new adventure. Papa John's was a great franchise, and I was back into what I did best: negotiating deals. Robin was a wonderful partner and often came with me to business meetings. She said she loved watching me in action, and I loved having her there. We were a great team.

Chapter 20

Robin was busy with the house—arranging furniture when it was delivered, hanging pictures, and shopping for everything we needed to make it our home. She began to complain about pain in her neck again and frequent headaches that seemed to never go away. Robin attributed the pain to the time she was spending hanging pictures and thought the disc problem she had several years earlier had returned. I finally encouraged her to see a doctor in Rancho Mirage and find out what was going on. I hated when Robin wasn't feeling well, and I knew she was in quite a bit of pain.

Robin saw an oncologist, who sent her for some tests so that he could make a diagnosis. I went with Robin to the hospital and waited while they ran a battery of tests. Of course, we had no idea what they'd found until we were summoned to the doctor's office to get the results. The doctor began speaking slowly, going over the test results with us. While I didn't understand all of the medical language, his demeanor was tense, his expression was serious, and my blood began to run cold. I knew what he was telling us was not good, and I feared what would come out of his mouth next. Then he said it in plain English: Robin had stage-four cancer. They couldn't be certain of the cancer's origin, but the original cancer had metastasized, and it was everywhere: in her brain, breast, liver, and bone. The cancer was so advanced that she had tumors everywhere, and there was nothing they could do that would save her life.

There are moments in life when time stands still. This was one of them. Neither Robin nor I could move or speak for some time. Was it seconds? Minutes? I don't know. All I know was that the doctor's words were trying to get through to my brain, but I couldn't absorb what he had said. Robin was dying? The words hung in the air with nowhere to go; they were words that neither of us was willing to hear, and a cold reality that we didn't want to know. Shock saves you, I guess, because your mind and body disconnect, and nothing seems real after that. Dying—was that really what he had said?

I looked at Robin. She was composed, but the tears had started to come. I didn't know what to say or do. I do know the rest of the time with the doctor is a blank in my mind. I have no idea what any of us said or did, how the appointment ended, or how we got home. I just know that suddenly, we were home, and our lives were no longer our lives but some surreal nightmare. We cried, we talked, and we cried again, but the buckets of tears we shed over the next few days could not erase the devastating news we had heard. Time, life's most precious commodity, was going to run out. I was going to lose my Robin, and she was going to lose her life. If I could have spent every dollar I had ever earned to buy her more time, I would have. I have never felt more helpless.

I called Hector to let him know the news and to say that I would not be coming in for the duration of Robin's illness. I told him he would have to run the company, as I needed to be with Robin to care for her and spend whatever time we had left together. Hector understood. I knew the company was in good hands and would continue to do well with Hector in charge. Strangely, it was easy to let go. Somehow, business wasn't important anymore; I had more-urgent things to attend to.

Robin and I tried to continue our normal lives, and we did for several months. We made an effort to get out of the house to play golf, shop, or go to dinner as often as we could. Robin began radiation and chemotherapy—not to be cured but to buy her more time. I went to all of her medical appointments and sat with Robin during her treatments. The chemotherapy made her sick, and the first twenty-four hours after the treatments was brutal. She often was up all night, and I tried to help any way I could. By morning, we were both exhausted. When Robin lost her hair, I went shopping and surprised her with several beautiful wigs. I had always loved buying Robin beautiful things: clothes, shoes, jewelry, cars—and now wigs. She couldn't have been more pleased to have them. How our lives had changed!

I was always with Robin when she got radiation treatments on her brain. She went into the MRI machine, and the images of her brain showed up on a screen so that the doctor could monitor her brain tumors and the effectiveness of the treatments. One day, the radiation oncologist invited me over to the screen so that I could see the images myself. I'll never know why she did that, because the news was not good. When I looked at the images, I could see the tumors were everywhere. It made me sick, and I had to look away. It is an image that haunts me to this day. Robin was not getting better, and what I saw confirmed it.

Our doctor suggested an experimental drug that he thought might help slow the progression of Robin's cancer, but he wasn't sure if we could get it. I called the insurance company, who promptly told me the drug was not available to us. After several attempts to get through to someone who might be able to help us, I became angry. My wife was dying, and even though this drug was a long shot, I was desperate to get her anything that might give her a chance. I had already offered to donate any organ I had to Robin, even if it meant losing my life. At sixty-eight, I felt I already had lived a good life, but Robin was only forty-seven and still had many years she could enjoy. The doctors could not allow me to sacrifice my life for hers and promptly rejected my offer. I would have if they'd let me, but now this drug was Robin's only chance. I called the insurance company one last time, and when they rejected me again, I asked for the name of the doctor who was denying us the drug. I told the woman on the phone, "I need the doctor's name, as I am not going to just sue your insurance company—I am going to sue the doctor who is making this decision!"

The drug was finally approved for Robin, and the insurance company even paid for the drug. Unfortunately, we knew it was a long shot, and the experimental treatment also failed to halt the progression of Robin's cancer.

Finally, we made the decision to stop all Robin's treatments and allow her to live out the rest of her days peacefully. Robin, who had never been a large woman, had lost a great deal of weight and had become weak. We brought in a hospital bed so that she wouldn't fall out of bed and hurt herself. I turned down the offer of hospice care, as I wanted to care for Robin myself as long as I could. Many days, I would carry Robin to our front porch, where she would sit in the sun and enjoy being outdoors. She spent much of the time praying, and I know it helped her. She certainly handled her illness and what lay ahead better than I did. We'd talk, and she'd say, "Wally, when I'm gone, you need to find someone who makes you happy and go on with your life." I couldn't imagine life without Robin and didn't want to hear it. Eventually, Robin became so weak that she needed to have someone with her twenty-four hours a day. I called hospice, and they provided a hospice nurse who stayed with Robin while I slept.

On October 15, 2001, Robin passed peacefully in her sleep. I was glad Robin no longer had to suffer, but without Robin, I was lost. I arranged to have Robin's body flown back to Colorado to be buried next to her mother, and I got in my car and drove twenty-two hours straight to get home. My daughter Cathy and her husband, Doug, stayed on the phone with me the whole way back to make sure I was okay. The days between my arrival and the funeral are a blur. Family and friends from all over the country came to attend Robin's funeral and offer me support. I was touched when Hector Ortiz and his wife showed up unexpectedly from LA, as he had not mentioned they would be there. I moved through those first weeks as if in a trance. I was numb and, although brokenhearted, was having difficulty feeling anything at all.

After a time, I went back to Rancho Mirage, but my heart wasn't in it. PJ Management Inc. was something that Robin and I had done together. She had been with me from my first conversations with our partners, Larry and Charles, at the Kemah Country Club, and once we'd made the decision to come out of retirement, everything we'd done, we'd done together. It was painful to be back in our home without Robin. Chuck Schnatter from Papa John's called within weeks of the funeral to let me know that the company expected me to continue opening new stores in my territory. He might have been frustrated and trying to encourage me to get back to work, but it was too soon for me, and when Chuck threatened to take the territory back if I didn't open new stores, I angrily told him they could have their territory back.

Hector continued to oversee the operation of the sixteen stores I already had open, which allowed me to take some time to figure out what I wanted to do next. A number of friends encouraged me to not sell the house or move for a few years, but I could not take their advice. After eighteen months, I put the house up for sale and bought a home back in Fort Collins, Colorado, where I continue to live. I eventually sold our home in Kemah, Texas, through a broker. The broker and our maid packed up our personal belongings and shipped them to me so that I would not have to go back to Texas. I sold our townhome in Phoenix and later bought another townhome for me to use as a winter getaway. I could not bring myself to live in any of the homes Robin and I had shared. It was too painful for me, and I knew I would have to move on with my life without her. Four years later, I sold my Papa John's stores to an investor for seven figures and have been fully retired ever since.

Years before Robin died, I set up skip-a-generation irrevocable trusts for Robin and my children. I put half of our assets in a trust for Robin, and the rest went to my children. Trusts are a good way to safeguard assets should something unexpected happen. I assumed that being older, I would be the one to go first, and I wanted Robin to be set for life. She would have been; the money can be used tax free for the life of the trustee. If there is money left to pass on, the next generation is responsible for the taxes. It is a smart way to protect assets should a tragedy occur. I had done my homework and thought I had all my bases covered, and I did financially. However, I never expected the curveball—Robin dying before I did. The day I got Robin's trust back was a difficult day—probably the only time in my life that a significant amount of money came my way that I wasn't happy to have.

Chapter 21

No one's life is perfect. We all experience the high and low moments in life, and I have had plenty of both. All of my business success and financial security did not make me immune to heartache and pain. Unfortunately, pain is part of the human condition we all share.

However, I feel incredibly blessed to have been given the opportunities I have had and to live a life that was beyond my imagining when I was a young man just starting out. I don't know what Don Small saw in me all those years ago. I walked into a meeting to try to get some investment bankers to invest in a bowling alley; I walked out with a job offer. That day—that moment—stands out in my memory as the moment one man literally changed my life. What I learned from Don Small and the investment banking business served me well, not only while I was working for Don but also in every negotiation and business deal in all the years that followed. He is the reason that I am now comfortably retired and able to do whatever I want without ever worrying about finances. In the nine years since I fully retired, I haven't had to touch any capital; rather, I can live well on the growth and interest of my investments. I worked hard for fifty years, but I would have worked hard no matter what job or career I eventually found, most likely without the same financial success. Was it luck? Fate? I don't know. What I am sure of, however, is that I never would have gotten this far if Don Small had not taken a chance on a young man who had nothing to offer but determination, a desire to learn, and the willingness to work hard. I still often wonder what he saw in me and why I got the chance to succeed. A chance was all I needed, and everything I have accomplished started with that.

Unfortunately, I have carried the pain of my childhood with me for more than seventy years. Ironically, that pain also provided me with my determination and drive to succeed; it was a double-edged sword, I guess. Once I became successful in business, I tried many times to help my parents, hoping that by doing so, I could create some kind of family for myself. I shouldn't have bothered, as every encounter just served as a reminder of their dysfunction and inability to see beyond themselves.

When my mother passed away, I did not attend her funeral, having finally accepted that while she gave me life, she gave me little else. Life, though, has been good, and I am thankful that my genetic inheritance allowed me to become who I am, parents who cared or not.

I became a father at twenty-one and tried hard to be the father I never had. I loved all my children, and having a family to support was never a burden but, rather, a motivator for me. I wanted my wife and children to feel safe and secure and to know that I would always be there to provide for them. Lorrie and I were just two young kids ourselves when we started out, and at the beginning, we had no idea that financial security would ever be possible for us. I didn't know what I was good at or what I wanted to do. I had little education and couldn't even dream about having a career. I just wanted a job and a paycheck, and once I had that, I would make the best of every opportunity I was given. I think I did that. I knew I wasn't stupid, even though I felt that way when I left school in the tenth grade. However, I learned something every day in every job I ever had. I also learned that to get ahead, you have to outwork, outthink, and outperform the people around you, or you'll be left behind. I was coming from behind, and it was a place I was determined to leave. The challenge was to figure out how. Every time I figured out how to do something I didn't know before, I felt a sense of accomplishment, and each time I had that feeling, I gained confidence that I could make it. I know I was naive, but not knowing that the odds were against me allowed me to believe that I could do anything I set my mind to. I knew if I didn't believe in myself, no one else would.

I had two marriages lasting more than twenty years. Lorrie and I raised our family together, she in the traditional role of homemaker and I in the role of the breadwinner. Lorrie was a great mother, and she supported every decision I made for us: packing up and moving when necessary, and living in whatever home we could afford. In the early days, it wasn't much. I will always be grateful that she trusted I would provide for our family. I never wanted to let my family down. I was often on the road in those early years, and she took good care of our family while I was away. We came a long way during our years together.

Sandy, Larry, Michael, and Cathy provided me the opportunity to create what I never had growing up: a family. Knowing that they depended on me was the only reason I needed to get out there and hustle. I wanted them to be able to experience childhood in a way I never could. Some of my favorite memories are of our Christmases together, when their eyes would light up at the boatload of presents Santa brought. Through them, I was able to have those moments I'd never had as a child. Was I a perfect father? Probably not—not because I didn't try but because I had no role model to follow. I did the best for them that I could and am proud of who they all have become in their own lives.

Everyone should be blessed to have a love of a lifetime. It is a relationship that is so special and rare that many people never get to experience it. Robin was that person for me. We never left each other's side from the moment we met until the day she died twenty-one years later. We lived the good life together, and I cherish every memory of our time together. I will never stop missing her.

So who am I? Am I poor, uneducated, shy, embarrassed, angry, and hurt? Or am I wealthy, knowledgeable, confident, outgoing, and proud? I am the sum total of all of these, so just call me Wally.

Is there a secret to success? Yes, there is. You can find it in the voice inside you that tells you, "You are better than this." Listen to that voice. It doesn't matter whether you started life with the same kinds of challenges I had or came upon your challenges later. The challenges will find you; they always do. But listen—you are better than this. Make that statement true. No one can do that for you; you have to do it yourself. Get all the education you can, and then get going. If you have a safety net, leave it behind. You will not suddenly get motivated if you are waking up in your childhood bed with your parents supporting you. To be hungry enough to succeed, you sometimes have to be literally hungry and even scared. Take any job you can find, and make the most of it. Then find another. Experience counts. Watch and learn from others every day. Buy only what you can afford, pay your bills, reinvest profits, don't burn bridges, stay focused, and believe in yourself. The only bounds are those you create for yourself. Believe me, there are no bounds.

www.ingramcontent.com/pod-product-compliance
Lightning Source LLC
Chambersburg PA
CBHW030809180526
45163CB00003B/1200